22.95

D0912904

DEMCO

The
Brain and
Nervous
System

Understanding
THE HUMAN BODY

The Brain and Nervous System

Titles in the Understanding the
Human Body series include:

Understanding
THE HUMAN BODY

The
Brain and
Nervous
System

Pam Walker and Elaine Wood

LUCENT BOOKS®

THOMSON

™

GALE

San Diego • Detroit • New York • San Francisco • Cleveland • New Haven, Conn. • Waterville, Maine • London • Munich

On Cover: The brain is responsible for all bodily functions and human
behaviors, including the creativity demonstrated by this artist.

LIBRARY OF CONGRESS CATALOGING-IN-PUBLICATION DATA

Walker, Pam, 1958–
          The brain and nervous system / by Pam Walker and Elaine Wood.
          p. cm. — (Understanding the human body)
Summary: Discusses the structures, functions, and mysterious operations of
the brain and nervous system.
Includes bibliographical references and index.
          ISBN 1-59018-148-4 (hardback : alk. paper)
     1. Nervous System—Juvenile literature. 2. Brain—Juvenile literature.
[1. Brain. 2. Nervous system.] I. Wood, Elaine, 1950– II. Title. III. Series.
          QP361.5 .W35 2003
          612.8—dc21

                                                                        2002004109

Printed in the United States of America

CONTENTS

FOREWORD

Since Earth first formed, countless creatures have come and gone. Dinosaurs and other types of land and sea animals all fell prey to climatic shifts, food shortages, and myriad other environmental factors. However, one species—human beings—survived throughout tens of thousands of years of evolution, adjusting to changes in climate and moving when food was scarce. The primary reason human beings were able to do this is that they possess a complex and adaptable brain and body.

The human body is comprised of organs, tissue, and bone that work independently and together to sustain life. Although it is both remarkable and unique, the human body shares features with other living organisms: the need to eat, breathe, and eliminate waste; the need to reproduce and eventually die.

Human beings, however, have many characteristics that other living creatures do not. The adaptable brain is responsible for these characteristics. Human beings, for example, have excellent memories; they can recall events that took place twenty, thirty, even fifty years earlier. Human beings also possess a high level of intelligence. Their unique capacity to invent, create, and innovate has led to discoveries and inventions such as vaccines, automobiles, and computers. And the human brain allows people to feel and respond to a variety of emotions. No other creature on Earth has such a broad range of abilities.

Although the human brain physically resembles a large, soft walnut, its capabilities seem limitless. The brain controls the body's movement, enabling humans to sprint, jog, walk, and crawl. It controls the body's internal functions, allowing people to breathe and maintain a heartbeat without effort. And it controls a person's creative talent, giving him or her the ability to write novels, paint masterpieces, or compose music.

Like a computer, the brain runs a network of body systems that keep human beings alive. The nervous system relays the brain's messages to the rest of the body. The respiratory system draws in life-sustaining oxygen and expels carbon dioxide waste. The circulatory system carries that oxygen to the body's vital organs. The reproductive system allows humans to continue their species and flourish as the dominant creatures on the planet. The digestive system takes in vital nutrients and converts them into the energy the body needs to grow. And the immune system protects the body from disease and foreign objects. When all of these systems work properly, the result is an intricate, extraordinary living machine.

Even when some of the systems are not working properly, the human body can often adapt. Healthy people have two kidneys, but, if necessary, they can live with just one. Doctors can remove a defective liver, heart, lung, or pancreas and replace it with a working one from another body. And a person blinded by an accident, disease, or birth defect can live a perfectly normal life by developing other senses to make up for the loss of sight.

The human body adapts to countless external factors as well. It sweats to cool off, adjusts the level of oxygen it needs at high altitudes, and derives nutritional value from a wide variety of foods, making do with what is available in a given region.

Only under tremendous duress does the human body cease to function. Extreme fluctuations in temperature, an invasion by hardy germs, or severe physical damage can halt normal bodily functions and cause death. Yet, even in such circumstances, the body continues to try to repair itself. The body of a diabetic, for example, will take in extra liquid and try to expel excess glucose through the urine. And a body exposed to extremely low temperatures will shiver in an effort to generate its own heat.

Lucent's Understanding the Human Body series explores different systems of the human body. Each volume describes the parts of a given body system and how they work both individually and collectively. Unique characteristics, malfunctions, and cutting edge medical procedures and technologies are also discussed. Photographs, diagrams, and glossaries enhance the text, and annotated bibliographies provide readers with opportunities for further discussion and research.

Structures and Functions of the Nervous System

The song title "No Man Is an Island" speaks volumes about the way humans live. Very few individuals spend their lives alone; most live and work with others in organized social groups. In organizations, individuals work together to accomplish common goals. Communication is the key to success within any organization. Unless individuals within a group stay in touch, they cannot work together efficiently.

The human body is an organization; it is made of millions of components that work together. Communication between parts is vital, and the body has an arrangement that is dedicated to carrying messages from one point to another—the nervous system. Within this highly complex information system there are specialized areas; some collect information from the environment, some assess that information, and others respond to it.

No man-made communication system can compare in complexity to the human nervous system. This exceptional design enables a person to perform millions of functions, such as thinking, talking, walking, and planning. The components of this communication and control system include the brain, the spinal cord, and an enormous network of nerves. More than 10 billion nerve cells extend throughout the body, connecting each tissue to the brain, to other nerves, and to each other.

Building Blocks of the Nervous System

The nervous system transmits information by means of nerve cells called neurons. These highly specialized cells hold the distinction of being the longest cells known to biologists. They are also among the oldest cells; unlike other body cells, many nerve cells never divide and replace themselves, so they are designed to last a lifetime. These long-lived cells vary tremendously in size. Some are so short that hundreds of them lined up end-to-end would not cross the diameter of a pinhead. Others are an astonishing three feet long.

Even though they have distinctive features, neurons share a lot of characteristics with other types of cells. For example, they are made mostly of cytoplasm, a thick, gelatin-like substance. Suspended within the cytoplasm of neurons are other basic structures that act in concert, like the components of a factory complex. A cell membrane surrounds each factory building like a fence, controlling what enters and leaves. There is an office in each factory building, too: the nucleus, a command post

Two nerve cells. Although similar to other human cells, neurons possess highly specialized characteristics.

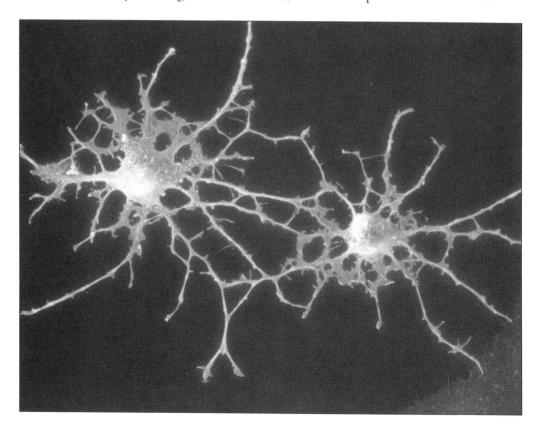

containing information to run the cell. The power generators of a cell that take in raw materials and convert them to energy are specialized units called mitochondria. The traffic within a cell passes along a series of hallways known as the endoplasmic reticulum. A complex entity called the Golgi apparatus receives material passing through the hallways and prepares it for export. Proteins, molecules that are both exported and used internally for cell structure, are built by ribosomes, which are comparable to the machinery of a manufacturing plant. A cell also has storage spaces represented by areas called vacuoles, and "support beams" in the form of microtubules.

Because nerve cells have the unique job of carrying information from one place to another, they have some distinctive features. Most notable of all neuron specializations are the fingerlike extensions of cytoplasm that stretch out from the cell body to receive or transmit information. These extensions, called dendrites, act like antennae for neurons, receiving information from the environment. The information received by a dendrite travels to the body of the neuron, then out through an axon, another cellular extension, which acts as an output zone. A nerve cell can have one or several dendrites, but only one axon.

Bundles of neurons grouped together as fibers run throughout the body. To the naked eye, they look like long, white threads. Their color is due to the fact that axons of many nerve cells are covered with a white, fatty material called myelin. Myelin acts like insulation on an electric wire; it protects the axon and speeds transmission of information. If myelin is missing or damaged, information is not carried along the nerve in a timely matter. When myelin is missing on nerves that connect to muscles, muscle movements are uncoordinated. The movements of newborns are jerky because myelin is still forming on the axons of their nerve cells. Alcohol, some other drugs, and some diseases destroy myelin around axons and affect muscle movements.

Support Cells

Neurons are not capable of functioning alone. They need the assistance of supportive neuroglial cells. These neuroglia are

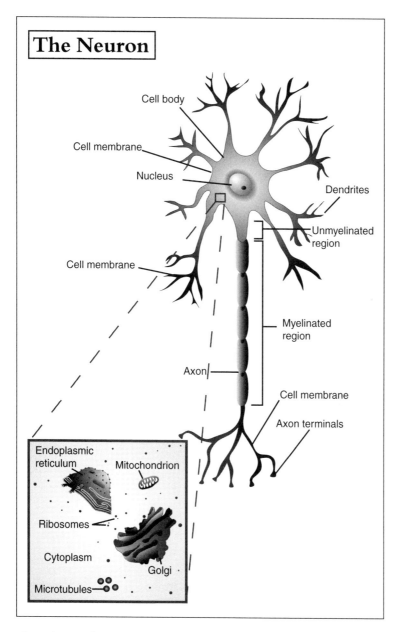

The Neuron

Cell body

Cell membrane

Nucleus

Dendrites

Unmyelinated region

Cell membrane

Myelinated region

Axon

Cell membrane

Axon terminals

Endoplasmic reticulum

Mitochondrion

Ribosomes

Cytoplasm

Golgi

Microtubules

abundant, taking up about half the volume of cells in the nervous system. Even though these cells resemble the neurons they support, neuroglia have very different jobs. Whereas neurons carry nerve impulses, neuroglia do not. And unlike neurons, neuroglia are able to divide and make more cells.

One of the jobs of neuroglia is to form a foundation on which neurons can grow. These cells develop into scaffolds that both prop up neurons and anchor them to supplies of nutrients. Neuroglia also wrap tightly around brain capillaries, creating a protective mechanism called the blood-brain barrier. Only very small molecules, like oxygen, water, carbon dioxide, and alcohol can reach brain cells by diffusing from blood through neuroglia; large molecules cannot penetrate. This prevents neurons in the brain from being exposed to any chemicals that might be traveling in the circulatory system.

The Information Highway

Neurons carry information through the body in the form of electrical impulses. These impulses move in one direction: from the axon of one nerve cell to the dendrite of another. Electrical impulses can fly along nerve fibers at lightning speeds of 260 miles per hour.

There are electrical charges both inside and outside a neuron's cell membrane, but the charge on the inside is never the same as the charge on the outside. When a neuron is resting, the fluid outside the cell membrane contains more positively charged particles than the fluid within the cell membrane. The difference in concentration of charged particles creates a small electrical charge known as a resting potential. The resting potential of a cell can be thought of as a capacity for activity along the membrane.

A nerve impulse begins when a stimulus such as pressure or light strikes a neuron. The stimulus opens gate-like pores in the cell membrane, allowing positively charged particles to rush into the cell and negatively charged particles to flow out. For a millisecond, the charges across the cell's membrane are reversed: There are more positively charged particles inside the cell membrane than out. This reversal of charges caused by the temporary change in polarity in the nerve-cell membrane is called an action potential. It starts a nerve impulse.

Once created, an action potential stimulates adjoining areas of cell membrane, causing their gates to open. As a result, action potentials move quickly from one point to another along the cell membrane, like a series of falling dominoes. When an action potential has passed, the cell membrane gates close. The membrane returns to its normal, resting state, ready to receive another stimulus.

Strange Connections

An action potential that has traveled the entire length of a neuron reaches the end of the road at the tip of the axon. It cannot travel directly from the neuron to the next cell because neuronal dendrites do not touch other cells. There is a gap called a synapse between a neuron and its neighbor. The cell carrying an impulse to a synapse is the presynaptic cell; the postsynaptic cell follows a synapse. Nerve cells form synapses with other neurons as well as with other types of cells, such as muscle and gland cells.

The axon of a neuron (large circular area in center) forms a synapse with a muscle fiber (dark area at left). The synaptic cleft is visible between them.

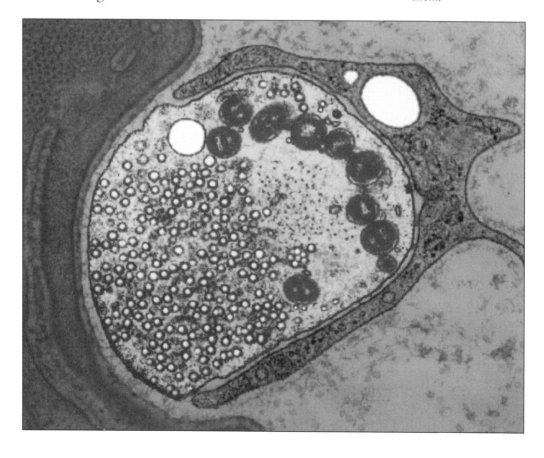

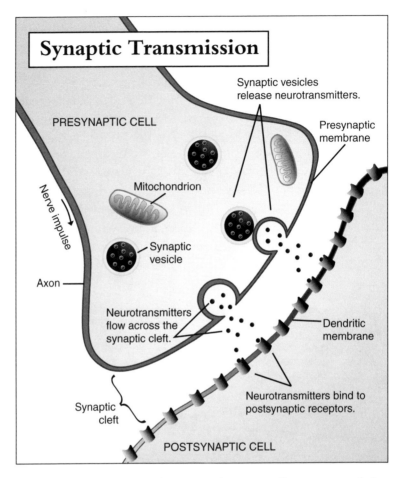

Synaptic Transmission

Synaptic vesicles release neurotransmitters.

PRESYNAPTIC CELL

Presynaptic membrane

Mitochondrion

Nerve impulse

Synaptic vesicle

Axon

Neurotransmitters flow across the synaptic cleft.

Dendritic membrane

Synaptic cleft

Neurotransmitters bind to postsynaptic receptors.

POSTSYNAPTIC CELL

Even though the gap between the axon of a neuron and the next cell is narrow—not even half the width of a cell—an action potential cannot jump across it. It must be carried across this space (the technical term is cleft) by chemicals. When an action potential arrives at a synapse, it stimulates little storage sacs, or vesicles, in the axon to open. The sacs release chemicals called neurotransmitters that flow quickly from the axon of the neuron across the synapse, where they bind to special receptors in the dendritic membrane of the next cell. This binding stimulates the postsynaptic cell, causing cell membrane pores to open and creating an action potential. It is this sequence of precisely controlled events that allows nerve impulses to pass beyond the neurons in which they originated.

After neurotransmitters carry an impulse across the synapse, they are not left in that space. They are either quickly removed by complex proteins called enzymes or reabsorbed into the axon for recycling so that another message can cross the space. There are more than sixty different molecules that act as neurotransmitters at synapses. Acetylcholine is an important neurotransmitter produced by neurons that attach to muscle cells.

Serotonin is a neurotransmitter produced by neurons in the brain. It affects brain cells by causing sleep. Another neurotransmitter in the brain is norepinephrine, a chemical that affects areas in the brain that regulate emotional states. Some of the other neurotransmitters that play key roles in transmission of signals in the brain are glutamate, dopamine, and gamma-aminobutyric acid (GABA).

Major Divisions of the Nervous System

Throughout the body, all of the individual nerves with their axons, dendrites, and synapses work together. The various parts of the nervous system operate as one big functional unit. However, for purposes of study, the nervous system is usually subdivided into two anatomical divisions: the central nervous system and the peripheral nervous system. The central nervous system includes the brain and spinal cord, two centers of nerve cells that receive information from nerves all through the body. The peripheral nervous system is made up of the nerves outside of the brain and spinal cord. Its job is to carry messages to and from the central nervous system.

The Brain at a Glance

The brain is the commander in chief of the body; it receives information, processes it, and responds appropriately. The spinal cord is an extension of the brain that connects it to spinal nerves. These two structures are the largest organs in the nervous system.

The brain of the average adult human male is a three-pound, white-and-gray mass whose surface resembles a walnut. It is made up of an estimated 100 billion neurons and 900 billion supportive neuroglia. Neurons in the brain are only able to divide to make new cells during fetal development and for a few months after birth. After that, no new brain cells are formed, although the ones in place increase in size until the age of eighteen years.

The brain has many different sections, all of which have distinct functions. When observing the brain, four anatomical areas can be seen. Beginning at the base and moving upward, these areas are the brain stem, cerebellum, diencephalon, and cerebrum.

The Brain Up Close

The brain stem, located at the base of the skull, is about three inches long and the approximate width of a thumb. It connects the rest of the brain to the spinal cord. Many of the neurons in the brain stem are pathways by which sensory information travels to the brain. Others are vital for survival because they control basic functions such as rate and depth of breathing, diameter of blood vessels, and rate of heartbeat. Injury or disease to this part of the brain often results in death. Other neurons in the brain stem control reflexes, such as constriction and dilation of pupils, and nonvital functions, like sneezing, hiccupping, and coughing. The brain stem houses several structures, including the medulla, pons, and the midbrain. These structures regulate body functions, jobs that are carried out without thought and are considered to be part of the unconscious brain. Extending through the entire brain stem is a diffuse mass called the reticular formation. The reticular formation plays important roles in consciousness and in cycles of sleep and wakefulness.

Beside the brain stem is the cerebellum, or cauliflower-shaped "little brain." It has two distinct halves and a wrinkled surface. Its functions relate to posture, muscle tone, movement, and balance.

The diencephalon sits on top of the brain stem and in front of the cerebellum. It contains two structures, the thalamus and hypothalamus. The thalamus relays information from the senses to appropriate parts of the cerebrum. The hypothalamus, which literally means "under the thalamus," responds to environmental changes that affect body temperature, hunger, thirst, and the body's own biological rhythm. The hypothalamus is also the location of the limbic system, or the emotional part of the brain, and therefore influences many urges and feelings. Within the limbic system are the amygdala and hippocampus. The amygdala influences social behavior in the very young, and to some extent social and sexual behavior in adults, whereas the hippocampus plays roles in both memory and learning.

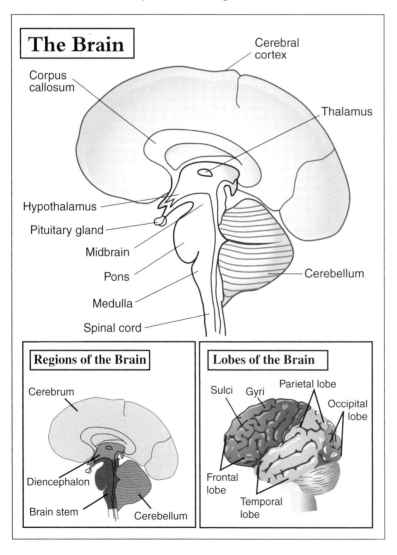

The Brain

Cerebral cortex

Corpus callosum

Thalamus

Hypothalamus

Pituitary gland

Midbrain

Pons

Cerebellum

Medulla

Spinal cord

Regions of the Brain

Cerebrum

Diencephalon

Brain stem

Cerebellum

Lobes of the Brain

Sulci Gyri Parietal lobe

Occipital lobe

Frontal lobe

Temporal lobe

The uppermost part of the brain is the cerebrum. If it were not pinched and folded to fit inside the skull in the familiar walnut configuration, the cerebrum would take up about as much space as two pages of newspaper. The outermost layer of the cerebrum, called the cerebral cortex, is made of cell bodies and thus has a gray appearance. Cortex comes from a Latin word meaning "bark." Underneath the gray cortex, the rest of the cerebrum is composed of white, myelin-coated axons and dendrites.

The cerebrum's surface is extremely convoluted, a mass of upward folds of tissue called gyri that are separated by grooves known as sulci. A deep groove divides the cerebrum into two halves, giving it the appearance of two boxing gloves lying side by side. The two sides, or hemispheres, of the cortex are connected by the corpus callosum, a band of nerve fibers.

Although most of the cerebrum's gray matter is located in the outer layer of tissue, some isolated patches of gray cell bodies are found deep within the white matter. These small islands, called basal ganglia, help coordinate movement and therefore play an important role in controlling the activities of skeletal muscles. Disorders that affect basal ganglia impair normal walking and other types of movements.

Cerebral Sections

Each cerebral hemisphere is divided into four distinct areas or lobes: occipital, temporal, parietal, and frontal. Even though all regions of the brain work together, each of these areas has specific jobs. The parietal lobe receives and deals with sensory input about pain, heat, cold, touch, taste, and pressure. A section of the parietal lobe in the back of the skull called Wernicke's area handles audio and visual information related to language.

Part of the frontal lobe is in charge of movement of muscles, so it is essential in motor skills. Another section, Broca's area, controls the lips, larynx, and cheek muscles that make sound. Therefore, Broca's area plays a critical role in speech.

Other parts of the frontal lobe are important in thought, memory, and learning. The occipital lobe receives and processes visual information, then sends it to the frontal and parietal lobes. The temporal lobe processes sound, then relays data to the parietal and frontal lobes.

The Brain's Protectors

Because it is delicate, the brain is protected in many ways. A strong outer covering of bone, the skull, shields it. Under the skull are three layers of membranes, or meninges. The outermost membrane, the dura mater, is made of tough, fibrous tissue that clings to the inside of the skull. The arachnoid membrane, which lies below the dura mater, is a delicate, weblike structure. The pia mater, or innermost membrane, is pierced with numerous tiny blood vessels. It fits snugly against the outer surface of the brain.

Within the brain are several cavities, or spaces, called ventricles. Clumps of pink tissue extend from the pia mater into these spaces. Cerebrospinal fluid (CSF), a protective liquid that bathes the entire central nervous system, seeps from these tissues into the ventricles but does not come in contact with the capillaries that supply the brain with blood. CSF flows into all areas of the brain, filling the spaces between meninges, and down around the spinal cord, thus helping to absorb shock.

Nerve Pathways

In adult humans, the spinal cord is a long, oval-shaped extension of the brain stem that stretches about seventeen inches down the back. Many of the nerve impulses traveling to and from the brain pass through the spinal cord. The spinal cord also serves as the center for nervous-system pathways called reflexes.

Like the brain, the spinal cord is surrounded by protective meninges and is bathed in shock-absorbing cerebrospinal fluid. It is further protected by a column of bones called vertebrae. Each vertebra is separated from the next by

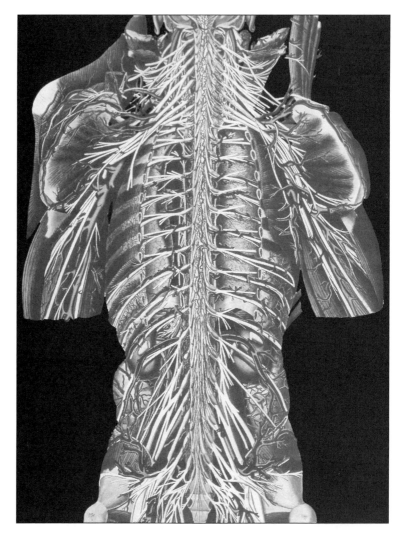

A computer-enhanced illustration displays nerves extending from the spinal cord. The brain and spinal cord comprise the central nervous system.

a disk of softer tissue, or cartilage, that helps cushion movement of the entire spinal column. An opening in each vertebra permits the extension of large spinal nerves from the spinal cord to various destinations throughout the body.

The Peripheral Nervous System

The peripheral nervous system is made up of all the nerves that are not part of the central nervous system; it includes millions of individual nerves and nerve fibers that extend through the body. Peripheral nerves serve as a highway for impulses traveling to and from the central nervous system. Sensory receptors at the ends of peripheral nerves collect information about the environment. These sensory receptors generate nerve impulses that travel along peripheral nerves, entering the central nervous system by large nerves extending from the spine and brain. The central nervous system analyzes information, then creates responsive nerve impulses. Different sets of peripheral nerves carry impulses from the brain to nerves that stimulate motor activities, such as muscle movement and stimulation of glands.

Some peripheral nerves do not travel all the way to the brain. Instead, they carry impulses in a circuit that begins in the environment, connects to the spine, then travels to a muscle or organ. This simple path of nerve conduction is called a reflex arc. Actions caused by reflexes do not require any thought; they happen quickly and predictably. Examples of reflex arcs include the production of saliva in the mouth when food is cooking and the quick removal of a hand that touches something hot.

Peripheral nerves connect to the central nervous system through cranial and spinal nerves. Cranial nerves are thick bundles of peripheral nerves that connect directly to the brain. They form twelve pairs of nerves that enter the brain through openings on each side of the skull. These connect the brain to nerves that affect speech, balance, hearing, smell, and vision, as well as activity of facial muscles. There are thirty-one pairs of spinal nerves that enter the central nervous system through the spinal cord. They provide communication between the spinal cord and various parts of the arms, legs, neck, and trunk.

Because the peripheral nervous system is large and complex, some scientists prefer to study its functions rather than its anatomy. All of the peripheral nerves can be classified into one of two divisions: the autonomic nervous system and the somatic nervous system. The autonomic nervous system contains nerves that are involved in controlling body activities. It is constantly fine-tuning the body through a variety of adjustments such as redistributing blood flow or changing

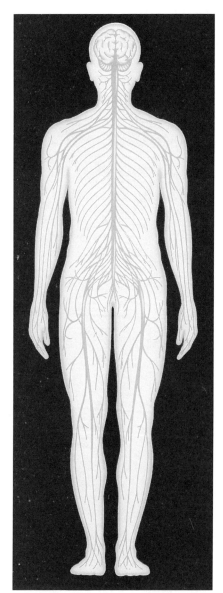

An illustration shows the peripheral nervous system. Peripheral nerves carry impulses to and from the brain and spinal cord.

heart rate. It primarily involves those nerve fibers that connect the central nervous system to organs, such as the lungs, heart, and stomach, and to glands, such as the pituitary and adrenal glands. Its name, autonomic, reflects the fact that most of its work is done automatically without conscious knowledge.

The Autonomic Nervous System

The autonomic nervous system has dual functions. Sometimes it speeds up organs and other times it slows them down. Therefore, this system can be studied as two subdivisions: the sympathetic system and the parasympathetic system. Most organs are supplied with nerve fibers from both. Nerve fibers from the sympathetic system stimulate organs, whereas nerve fibers from the parasympathetic system inhibit them. By working together, the two systems keep the organs balanced and functional.

In day-to-day life, it is unusual for one system to dominate; they usually work together. However, each specializes in preparing the body for different situations. The sympathetic system gets the body ready to expend energy. It is often thought of as the "fight or flight" system. During an emergency, it prepares the body to cope with a stressful situation by increasing such functions as heart rate, breathing, blood pressure, and levels of energy-supplying glucose in the blood. The sympathetic system dilates blood vessels so they can carry more blood to muscles, and it diverts blood flowing to digestive organs to the muscles.

On the other hand, the parasympathetic system is most active when the body is resting and is not threatened in any way. It is also called the "resting and digesting" or "housekeeping" system. Its primary concerns include normal digestion, elimination of wastes, and conservation of body energy. After an emergency, the parasympathetic system balances the effects of the sympathetic system by slowing heart and breathing rates, reducing blood pressure, sending blood back to digestive organs, and reducing glucose in the blood to a normal level.

The Somatic Nervous System

The somatic nervous system includes all nerves that respond to information collected by the senses—sight, hearing, taste, touch, and smell. There are millions of somatic nerves scattered throughout the body. If a sense organ detects a change in the environment, it relays that information to the brain. In turn, the brain responds and sends a signal along a somatic nerve to an appropriate skeletal muscle or organ. Because the somatic system stimulates muscles, including those used in voluntary activities, it is sometimes called the voluntary nervous system.

Responses by the somatic system involve both conscious and unconscious acts. For example, when a person is sitting on the beach in the bright sunlight, nerves in the eye send a message to the brain that the sun is bright. In response, somatic nerves carry a message to the eyelids, closing them partially to block out the sun. Like many somatic responses, this is an unconscious act. However, if the person decides to move to a shady area to avoid bright sunlight, the muscles that make that move possible are also part of the somatic system.

Nerves Control It All

Of all the body's organ systems, the nervous system may be the most complex. Made up of billions of individual nerve cells, its job is to provide communication between all parts of the body within milliseconds. To head up all its work, it is controlled by a central processing station called the brain.

This powerful command post reviews incoming stimuli, then reacts to them appropriately. The spinal cord and peripheral nervous system deliver messages to the brain and carry the brain's responses back to the appropriate tissues. Working every minute of every day, the nervous system maintains all body functions.

2 **The Senses**

Humans could not function without the brain, a mechanism for the overall management of neural activity. However, just as importantly, the nervous system cannot do its job unless it is supplied with information. It is somewhat like a computer; to operate, it must receive data. A diverse group of tissues generally described as the senses are responsible for providing this information. Just as data enters a computer through a keyboard, scanner, or camera, so information enters the nervous system through the senses. Sense organs collect information by responding to stimuli, or changes in the environment.

Any change in a human's internal or external environment will elicit a response, major or minor, from that person. Stimuli of all types, including chemicals, light, pressure, temperature, and sound, are introduced to the nervous system through sensory tissues and organs. Within these organs, specialized cells called receptors perceive stimuli of particular kinds and convert them into nerve impulses.

Sense organs are classified as general or special. The general senses are associated with touch, and they make humans aware of temperature, pain, and pressure. Receptors for general stimuli are scattered throughout the body, with concentrations in the skin, muscles, and joints. Special senses include sight, hearing, taste, and smell. The receptors for these senses are found in the large sense organs: the eye, ear, taste buds in the mouth, and olfactory receptors inside the nose.

The long cell pictured at center is an olfactory receptor, which is responsible for the sense of smell.

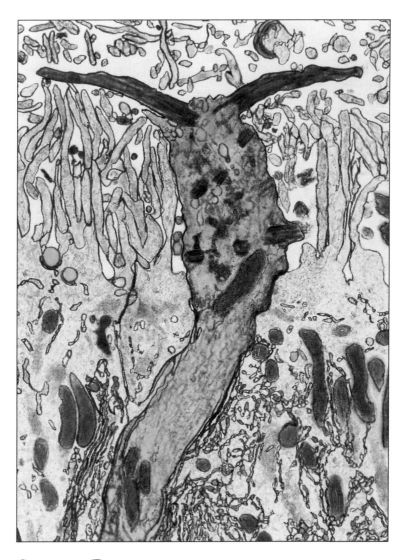

Sensory Receptors

When a receptor cell is stimulated by a change in the environment, an action potential develops in that cell's membrane. As a result, gate-like pores in the membrane open and charged particles rush into the cell, triggering the cell to discharge an electrical impulse. Impulses from sensory cells travel along nerves to the central nervous system. Some go directly to the brain, some travel to the brain by way of the spine, and others go straight to the spine. No matter what their path, signals that reach the brain are processed and in-terpreted. The brain responds to impulses by sending signals back to muscles or organs along tracts of nerves.

Within the brain, most incoming sensory signals travel first to the thalamus, a centrally located, egg-shaped struc-ture. From there, they proceed to the sensory regions of the cerebrum. However, some types of signals take different routes; those that help the body determine position or pos-ture travel first to the cerebellum then move on to the cere-brum. Signals related to the emotional aspects of pain enter the limbic system before traveling to the cerebrum.

Adaptation and Receptors

The sensory signals that travel to the brain are generated by stimulation of sensory receptors. To some degree, the more a sensory receptor is stimulated, the more it responds by sending additional messages to the brain. However, there is a limit to how much stimulation some receptors can tolerate. When exposed to the same stimulation over and over again, some receptors undergo an adjustment called adaptation.

When cells adapt to a continuous stimulus, the rate at which they produce electrical impulses slows compared to the rate at which they are stimulated. Eventually, cells may stop producing impulses altogether, even though the stimu-lation continues. A strong odor provides a good example of sensory adaptation. When a person enters a room where there is a very strong odor of perfume, the smell may be so pungent that it is annoying. However, after a time the odor becomes less and less noticeable. That is why people with jobs at foul-smelling workplaces do not notice the unpleas-ant aromas after a day or two.

Not all receptor cells can recognize the same kinds of stimuli. For example, sensory receptors in the ear are not stimulated by light. The types of receptor cells found in the sense organs and tissues can be classified according to the stimuli to which they are sensitive. Chemoreceptors respond to chemicals and play a role in the special senses of taste and smell. Pain receptors, found in the skin, muscles, and joints, respond to tissue damage. The skin contains thousands of thermoreceptors, which perceive different temperatures. Mechanoreceptors, which act in response to changes in pressure or the movement of fluids, are essential in the sense of hearing. Cells that perceive light are called photoreceptors and are responsible for vision.

The General Senses of Touch, Pressure, Temperature, and Pain

Touch is a complicated sensation that involves receptors to pressure, pain, heat, and cold. Not all areas of the body are covered equally by general receptors. For example, mechanoreceptors, which can detect pressure on tissues, are numerous on lips, fingertips, palms, soles, nipples, and external genitalia. However, mechanoreceptors on the back and neck are widely spaced.

Temperature receptors are found all over the skin; some are specialized for heat and others for cold. Warm temperatures cause warm-temperature receptors to discharge; the cooler the temperature, the more often the cold receptors discharge. Like other touch receptors, temperature-sensitive cells can adapt. That is why people get used to the hot water in a bathtub or the cold water of a pool.

Pain is an uncomfortable sensation that is produced when pain receptors in the skin and internal tissues are stimulated. Although pain receptors are located over most of the body, they are absent in the brain. That is why brain tissue does not experience pain. People undergoing brain surgery only need anesthesia on the scalp; they do not feel the probes and scalpels entering the soft tissue of the brain itself.

Feeling Pain

Pain receptors differ from other sensory receptors in an important way. Over time, they do not adapt. Continued stimulation causes continued pain. The receptors for pain can send signals to the central nervous system for a long period of time.

The ability to experience pain is actually a good thing. The sensation people feel when tissues are damaged has a protec-

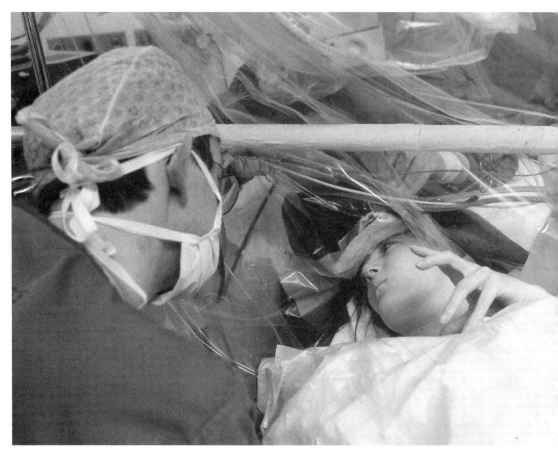

tive function. For example, if a person sticks their finger in a flame, a painful burning sensation lets the brain know to send a signal to the hand to move that finger. Thus, pain is a signal that something should be done to remove the source of stimulation. A small number of people are born without pain receptors, so they do not know when they are injured, unless, for example, they can see blood. Without the ability to sense pain, people with this rare condition are likely to allow minor injuries to become serious because they are unaware of initial damage.

Although the mechanisms of pain receptors are not completely understood, two theories are being studied by scientists. Both of these theories may have validity and may even entail separate parts of the same mechanism. One suggests

The brain does not contain pain receptors, allowing patients like this woman to remain awake during brain surgery.

that pain is related to the balance of information traveling to the spinal cord in two ways: along large nerve fibers and along small nerve fibers. When the amount of activity is greater along large nerve fibers, the brain does not receive a pain message. However, if there is more information traveling along small nerve fibers, the brain perceives pain. This theory explains why it feels good to rub a toe immediately after it has been stubbed. Large nerve fibers carry impulses from the rub, overwhelming the impulses of pain traveling along small nerve fibers.

Other research indicates that when tissue is injured, it releases chemicals. These chemicals have the ability to bind with and stimulate pain receptors in the body. These receptors send impulses to the brain that are interpreted as pain when they reach the thalamus.

The Eyes

Of all the sense organs, the eye, which is responsible for sight, has been studied the most. There are more sensory-receptor cells in the eye than in any other sense organ, and, indeed, the eyes are the largest sense organs. Each hollow sphere has a diameter of about one inch, but only one-sixth of the eye is visible in the front because most of it lies behind bone, fat, and muscle.

The sphere that forms the wall of the eye is made of three layers of tissue, and its interior is filled with fluids called humors. The outermost layer of the eye is the sclera, a strong, white tissue commonly called the white of the eye. In the front of the eyeball, the sclera is modified into a transparent area called the cornea. To protect itself, the cornea contains plenty of nerve endings, and so it is extremely sensitive. Irritation to the cornea stimulates blinking and the production of tears, two mechanisms that keep the front of the eye clean and prevent damage.

The clear cornea is structurally different from the white scleral tissue. It is made up of thin fibers that are arranged in unusually regular patterns. This neatly stacked tissue is transparent because these fibers contain very few cells and no blood vessels. Without blood vessels, there are not any immune-system cells in the cornea. Therefore, it is the only tissue that can be transplanted from one person to another without danger of rejection.

The middle section of the eye wall is the choroid layer, a blood-rich tissue that contains a lot of pigment. The role of pigment in the eye is to absorb any light waves that may scatter inside the eyeball. In the front, the choroid is customized as two smooth muscle structures: the ciliary body, which holds the lens, and the colored iris, which regulates the amount of light that enters the eye. The opening within the iris is the pupil.

The lens, a clear, flexible structure, is suspended in the middle of the pupil. When light waves enter the eye, the lens focuses them onto the retina. This flexible, convex structure

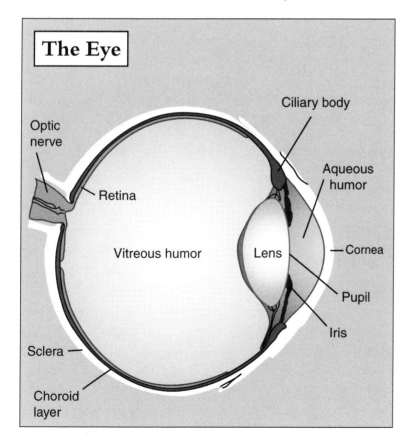

The Eye

Ciliary body

Optic nerve

Retina

Aqueous humor

Vitreous humor

Lens

Cornea

Pupil

Iris

Sclera

Choroid layer

is held in place by extensions of the ciliary body. In young people, the lens is transparent and easily bent. With age, it becomes more opaque and rigid.

The lens separates the eye into two chambers. The anterior chamber, which is in front of the lens, contains a clear, watery fluid called aqueous humor. The posterior chamber, behind the lens, is filled with a gel-like material called vitreous humor. These fluids help the eyeball maintain its shape.

The eye's innermost layer is the retina. Unlike the outer two layers, the retina does not cover the entire eye, only the

Rod and cone cells (pictured) are found in the retina. Rod cells detect light intensity; cone cells detect color.

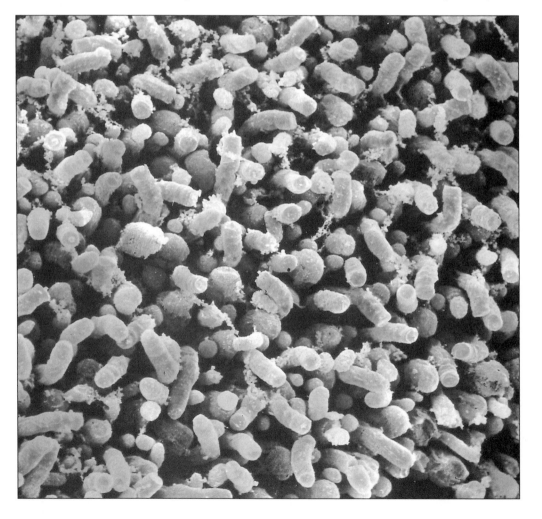

back. The retina is made up of a sheet of photoreceptor cells. In the back of the eye, the retina merges with the optic nerve.

Two types of photoreceptor cells, rods and cones, make up the retina. Each kind of cell has a different job. Rods, which are more sensitive to light than cones, enable people to see in relatively dim light. The images produced by rods are in black and white. Cones, which require bright light, confer the ability to detect color as well as black-and-white images.

The Act of Seeing

Vision depends on light waves. Only objects that give off or reflect light waves can be seen. When the light waves from an object enter the eye, they are bent by the cornea, lens, and fluids. The shapes of the cornea and fluids are always the same, so the degree to which they bend light waves is constant. However, the lens can change shape, so it plays a key role in focusing light. Its shape is controlled by the ciliary body, which can contract and force the lens to curve. The more convex the lens becomes, the more it bends light waves. Light waves entering the eye are bent and focused so that they project on the retina.

Both types of photoreceptors, rods and cones, work by the same basic mechanism. Each cell contains a pigment called rhodopsin, or visual purple, which breaks down when light hits it. The breakdown of rhodopsin releases an enzyme that starts a series of chemical reactions. The end result of these reactions is the opening of gates in the cell's membrane. When cell-membrane gates open, charged particles rush into the cell, creating a change in the electrical charges surrounding that cell's membrane and producing an electrical nerve impulse. The electrical impulse travels from the retina, along the optic nerve, and to the brain.

How the Ears Detect Sound

The ears, like the eyes, are large sense organs. These organs of hearing respond to the stimulus of sound waves. Sounds waves are produced by vibrating objects. The ears convert sound waves into electrical impulses that can travel along nerves to the brain.

Most of the ear is protected by bones of the skull. Only the outer ear, a flap of skin and cartilage called the pinna, and a short ear canal, are not contained deep within the skull. The pinna captures sound waves and funnels them into the ear canal. The canal ends at the eardrum, or tympanic membrane, a cone-shaped tissue that separates the outer ear from the middle ear. Modified sweat glands in the canal secrete cerumen, a waxlike material that catches insects, dust, and any other foreign matter before it can reach the eardrum.

The middle ear is a small, air-filled chamber that contains three tiny bones. Named for their shapes, the malleus (hammer), incus (anvil), and stapes (stirrup) form a bridge between the external and internal ear. The first of these, the malleus, connects directly to the eardrum. It is linked to the incus,

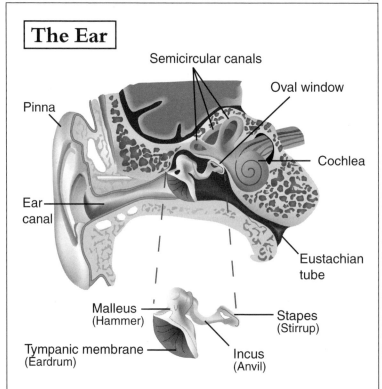

The Ear

Semicircular canals

Oval window

Pinna

Cochlea

Ear canal

Eustachian tube

Malleus (Hammer)

Stapes (Stirrup)

Tympanic membrane (Eardrum)

Incus (Anvil)

Source: U.S. National Library of Medicine website.

which in turn is attached to the stapes, which is the smallest bone in the human body.

For the eardrum to function correctly, air pressure in the middle and outer ear must be the same. If not, the eardrum cannot vibrate normally and hearing is impaired. Air reaches the middle ear through the Eustachian or auditory tube. This canal connects the middle ear to an area of the throat called the nasopharynx. Swallowing and yawning open the canal and allow air pressure inside and outside the ear to equalize. This prevents air pressure from building up inside the middle ear.

The stapes joins a small, membranous opening, the oval window, that leads to the inner ear. Because it has such a complicated shape, the inner ear is also called the labyrinth. Within this labyrinth are the organs of equilibrium and the cochlea. The fluid-filled cochlea, which looks like a snail's shell, is a hearing structure; it connects to the oval window.

Within the cochlea is the organ of Corti, a membrane containing thousands of tiny, stiff hairs of varying lengths. The membrane is so long that it wraps around itself two and one-half times to fit in its allotted space. Inside this structure, dendrites of nerve cells are located at the base of each hair.

The Sense of Hearing

The sensation of hearing is caused by a chain of events that begins with a sound. Sound waves enter the ear and travel along the ear canal to the eardrum, causing it to move back and forth. The eardrum, in turn, vibrates the malleus, incus, and stapes. The stapes vibrates the oval window, which creates waves in the fluid of the cochlea. Movement of cochlear fluid bends the sensitive hairs in the organ of Corti.

Depending on their pitch, different sounds affect different hairs. Those with lowest frequency activate the wide, more flexible hairs. The high frequency sounds set in motion the narrow, stiff hairs. Movement of each hair stimulates dendrites of neurons underneath them. The neurons generate electrical nerve impulses that travel to the auditory nerve. From there, they are relayed to the thalamus, then to the temporal lobe of the cerebral cortex, where they are interpreted as sound.

The Sense of Equilibrium

The sense of equilibrium involves several structures in the inner ear. Three fluid-filled semicircular canals, located next to the cochlea and lying at right angles to each other, play a role in equilibrium when the head is moving. Like the cochlea, each of these three pretzel-shaped canals contains tiny hairs. When the head changes position, fluid flows through the canals, brushing against the hairs and causing them to bend. Bending stimulates nerve endings, creating electrical signals that travel to the brain. These signals help determine orientation and position of the head. The brain responds automatically by sending signals to muscles that keep the body in its correct position.

The vestibule, located between the cochlea and semicircular canals, contains the organs that help maintain head position and posture when the body is not moving. The utricle and saccule are chambers within the vestibule. A section of the utricle contains hair cells that project upward into a gelatin-like material. Tiny "stones" of calcium carbonate are suspended in the gelatin to increase its weight.

When the head is bent forward, backward, or to one side, the stones and gelatin shift within the utricle. Movement of the heavy gelatin bends sensitive hair cells, triggering nerves of equilibrium. This is similar to the way movement of fluid in the cochlea stimulates nerves of hearing. The resulting nerve impulses travel to the brain. In response, the brain sends motor impulses to muscles in the head that help keep it in balance.

Smell and Taste

The tissues responsible for the senses of smell and taste are relatively simple compared to the complex eye and ear. Whereas hearing and vision are senses that are stimulated by energy, the organs that perceive smell and taste respond to chemicals. Tissues that form these two senses are located close together, and they complement each other. This is obvious when the nose is stuffy; smell is blocked and foods are often tasteless. As a team, these two senses

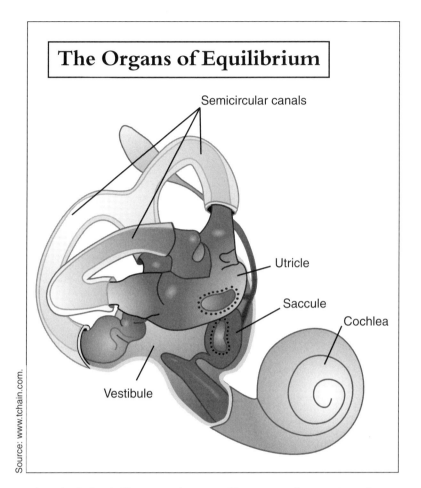

The Organs of Equilibrium

Semicircular canals

Utricle

Saccule

Cochlea

Vestibule

Source: www.tchain.com.

play slightly different roles in collecting information about chemicals. Olfactory tissues serve as an alert system; they have the ability to detect chemicals from a distance. Tissues that register taste must actually come in contact with chemicals to analyze them.

The cells responsible for smell, the olfactory tissues, cover an area no bigger than a postage stamp in the upper part of each nasal cavity. These receptors look like small, yellowish brown masses. They contain millions of neurons whose dendrites are covered with hairlike cilia. The cells and their cilia are kept moist by mucus that is secreted from glands underneath them. Airborne chemicals dissolve in the mucus before they come in contact with the cilia.

An odor is made of chemical molecules in the gaseous state. The way an odor stimulates an olfactory cell is not well understood. Most scientists believe that the cilia may contain receptor sites that are capable of binding with molecules. Binding of odor molecules to receptors may be the trigger that creates nerve impulses that travel to olfactory nerves, then to a portion of the limbic system in the brain. From there, impulses move to areas of the cortex in the temporal lobes and at the base of the frontal lobes. Because the limbic system is also involved in memory and emotion, some smells are linked to feelings from the past.

Olfactory tissues are located high in the nasal cavity, away from the usual path of inhaled air. To smell something that has a faint odor, a person may have to sniff and force air up to these receptors. Like many other sensory receptors, olfactory receptors undergo adaptation to a scent after a time. However, adaptation to one scent does not affect sensitivity to other odors.

Interpreting Tastes

Like cells of smell, those that interpret taste also respond to chemical stimuli. Taste cells are found in more than

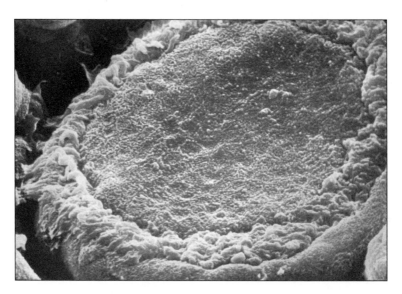

A miniscule human taste bud (pictured) contains fifty to one hundred taste cells.

ten thousand tiny tastes buds, located primarily on the tongue but also found on the roof of the mouth and the walls of the pharynx. Each onion-shaped taste bud contains fifty to one hundred taste, or gustatory, cells, the actual taste receptors. Most taste buds on the tongue are found in papillae, the tiny bumps that give the tongue its rough surface. The most noticeable are the papillae on the front of the tongue; each of these contains one or more taste buds.

Tiny projections called taste hairs, which are the sensitive portions of the cells, extend from the surface of each taste cell. Within a taste bud, nerve cells surround gustatory cells. When gustatory cells are stimulated, impulses are triggered on nearby nerve fibers. These travel directly through cranial nerves to the brain, where they are interpreted as taste.

Even though all taste buds look similar to the naked eye, four distinct types can be seen when they are examined under the microscope. Each type is most sensitive to one of the four taste sensations: sweet, sour, salty, and bitter. Each type of taste receptor is most highly concentrated in a specific region of the tongue. Some scientists believe that a fifth category, umami, is the sensation produced by glutamate, a constituent of protein found in meats, fish, and legumes. In any case, the sense of tasting reveals many attributes of a chemical stimulus other than flavor. It also indicates the intensity of the stimulus and whether or not it is pleasant or unpleasant.

When food or some other type of chemical is dissolved in saliva, it contacts the cilia on taste cells. Stimulation of cilia causes ion channels to open in the membranes of taste cells, creating electrical impulses in nearby nerve cells. These impulses travel on nerve fibers from receptors in the mouth to a portion of the brain called the medulla oblongata. From there, the impulses ascend to the thalamus, then travel to the gustatory cortex in the parietal lobe of the cerebrum.

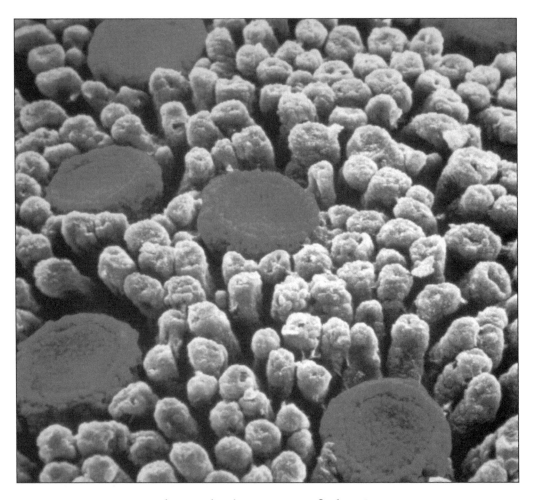

Minute projections called taste hairs cover the surface of the tongue. The round areas, called papillae, contain the taste buds.

The Whole Story of the Senses

The colors of a sunset, the sound of children laughing, and the warmth of the sun on the skin are just a few of the millions of sensations that humans experience. Everything about life is perceived through the senses. Sense organs link the nervous system to the body's internal and external worlds. Without information from the senses, the nervous system would be operating in the dark.

Any type of information that triggers a sense organ is called a stimulus. Each sense organ is especially equipped to turn a specific stimulus into a nerve impulse that travels to the brain. The eye and ear respond to energy stimuli, whereas taste buds and olfactory tissues interpret information from chemicals. Information about pressure, temperature, and pain are received and processed by touch receptors throughout the body.

Sense organs cannot do their jobs in isolation. Each depends on and works with the huge network of cells that make up the brain and the rest of the nervous system. Serving as portals for incoming information, the senses monitor internal body conditions and provide the nervous system with information about life.

Mysteries of the Brain: Sleep and Memory

3

Because the brain is the human body's most complex organ, scientists study it in many ways. Some scientists examine its physical structures, some its chemistry, and others its function. Yet, despite all the research, no one understands exactly how the brain and nervous system operate.

The human nervous system can carry out so many complicated functions that at times it almost seems magical. For centuries, scientists have tried to understand how it works. Much of the earliest work in neuroscience, the study of the nervous system, was done on the brains of dead animals and people. These specimens could only provide limited information because they had ceased to function. Today, technology helps scientists study nervous systems within living organisms.

Two fascinating and often-studied brain functions are memory and sleep. Each has been the object of much research in the field of neuroscience. Memory and sleep affect mental and physical health in ways that are just now being understood.

Memory

Memory provides each person with a record of the past. Knowing the past is essential to every human's individuality. Memory is such an integral part of existence that it is difficult to imagine living without it. If memory were absent, a person could not recall what had been said to them from one minute to the next. Without a way to store information in the brain, learning would be impossible. A person with no memory would not be able to access basic information such as whether or not they have recently eaten a meal or where they live.

Scientists have attempted to liken memory to some man-made device for comparison purposes. Some equate the memory to a library because it serves as a huge storehouse of information. Others compare memory to a computer because it can take in new information, review that information, then store it. However, memory is much more complicated than either of these man-made systems. One of the best descriptions was provided by a scientist who simply described memory as a "magic slate," with a surface on which new information can be recorded thousands of times

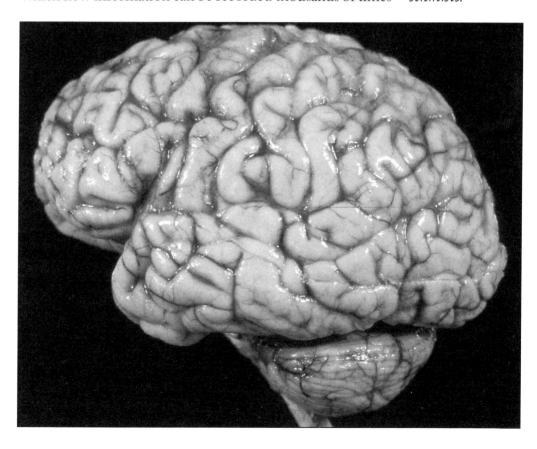

A human brain specimen. Despite years of research, many of the brain's complex functions still mystify scientists.

a day while still retaining much that was recorded there in the past.

Making Memories

Before something can become a memory, the brain must experience it. The brain constantly receives stimulation through the senses. For example, images are delivered to the brain through the eyes during every waking second. Similarly, sounds constantly flow to the brain through the sense of hearing. Information of all types bombards the brain through all the sense organs. Some of this sensory information is important and the brain needs to deal with it, but much of it is unessential.

Information from the sense organs must travel through an area called the sensory register when it enters the brain. This region acts as a waiting room for incoming data. It holds information for a fraction of a second so that the brain can evaluate it to see if it should be kept or deleted. Most sensory input is deleted. If it were not, the brain would be so overloaded by stimuli that it could not focus on any one thing.

Information that is not deleted in the sensory register moves into short-term memory. Short-term memory is a temporary storage area where information is held and evaluated further. The length of time that data stays in short-term memory varies; it may be held for as little as a minute or for as long as a few days.

Short-term memory can only retain six or seven units at one time. The numerals in a telephone number or the items on a short shopping list can be held in short-term memory. Most of the items that are admitted into short-term memory are eventually deleted.

Information moves from short- to long-term memory only if the brain makes an effort to retain it. To keep material, the mind must rehearse it or mark it as important. For this to happen, the brain focuses special attention on the item to be remembered, ignoring other sensory input while doing so.

Items in long-term memory can be retained for days, months, years, or throughout an entire lifetime. Long-term memory organizes and files an incredible collection of material, ranging from childhood images to the Gettysburg Address. It is long-term memory that maintains a person's knowledge about themselves and the world around them.

Where Is It?

One of the goals of scientists who study memory is to find the location in the brain where memories are made and stored. In the 1920s, one scientist devised a series of simple experiments with rats in order to determine the location of this place. First, he taught a group of lab rats how to find their way through a maze. Then he surgically removed a different section of brain from each rat. He reasoned that by systematically removing different parts of the rats' brains, in at least one of the rats he would remove the part of the brain that held the memory of the maze. When he placed the rats back in the maze after surgery, however, all of them could find their way to the end. It seemed that no matter what part of a rat's brain he removed, it could still remember its way through the maze. From this work, he suggested that memory is not located in one place, but is spread throughout the brain.

From this experiment and many others, scientists now know that memory is a very complicated brain function. The ability both to make a memory and store it requires many areas of the brain. Some memories are associated with smells, sights, and other sensations and use some of the same sections of brain as the senses. When memories are stored, the brain tags them with cues related to senses. That is why a walk beside the ocean or the smell of salty air can trigger a stream of memories about a past trip to the beach.

Cementing a Path

From the research such as that using sophisticated clinical imaging techniques and from experiments done on animals,

A patient undergoes an MRI scan, one of many sophisticated imaging techniques designed to see inside the body.

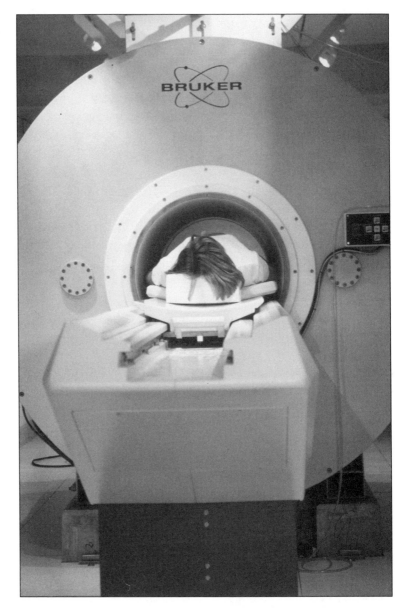

scientists generally agree on the mechanism that forms a memory. When an electrical impulse repeatedly travels along a chain of nerve cells, a memory is created. As impulses pass through the same neurons over and over again, those neurons create stronger and stronger connections at the points where they synapse. A continuous flow of electrical impulses along a pathway of neurons seems to cement the path. When the electrical activity slows down, the new connections remain intact. The path made by a short-term memory is formed quickly and is not as stable as the path created by a long-term memory.

Recent studies have shed new light on the formation of memories by showing which parts of the brain are active during certain tasks. In one experiment, people were shown and reshown a series of pictures, a process that allowed them to build visual memories. During this study, images acquired by means of a technique called magnetic resonance imaging (MRI) showed that two regions of the brain were very active: an area of cortex in the right frontal lobe and another near the hippocampus. By using magnetic resonance and other imaging techniques, scientists are beginning to understand the enormous complexity of memory formation.

Lost Memories

Another invaluable strategy for learning about memory is studying the case histories of people who have lost their memories. One of the most famous case histories came from work done in 1953. In that year, surgeons removed the hippocampus from the brain of an epileptic patient in an effort to stop his seizures. The results were drastic. The patient lost his ability to form new, or short-term, memories. However, he could still remember details from his distant past. This finding suggested to scientists that the hippocampus is needed to form short-term memories, but is not used in making long-term memories.

Confirmation of the role of the hippocampus in short-term memory came from a patient who contracted a viral infection in 2001. When the patient recovered, he found that he had lost his ability to form any new memories. However, when taken to the small town where he grew up, he could remember his classmates and find his way around town. Even though this patient lost his ability to form new memories, he was capable of recalling old ones. An MRI showed that the infection had destroyed his hippocampus.

How Does the Hippocampus Form Memories?

Knowing that the hippocampus is necessary for formation of memories, scientists are now trying to find out exactly what happens in this structure. Helpful information has been derived from animal studies that indicate the hippocampus may link together different pieces of information delivered to it by the senses. Evidence suggests that the hippocampus creates a detailed picture of any moment in time by using information delivered through a variety of sensory impulses. Within the hippocampus of rats, different kinds of sensory input, such as sights or smells, stimulate neurons that are lying next to each. Scientists believe that the brain pools the different pieces of information in these neurons to create a single picture or memory. Timing is critical here, because in order for several different sensory cues to be linked, they must arrive at the hippocampus at the same time. That is, for a group of sensory cues to be packaged together as a single memory, they must enter the hippocampus together.

Despite its key role in coordinating and collecting sensory cues, however, the hippocampus does not work alone. Other parts of the brain, including several areas of the cortex, are involved in linking information to create and preserve memories. Research helps doctors find new ways to treat diseases that affect the memory. Scientists hope to discover why some older people who are able to remember the past very clearly have extremely poor memories of recent events. New memory imaging techniques may be useful in predicting who is at risk for Alzheimer's disease, with its distressing symptoms of memory loss and deterioration in thinking ability.

Sleep

One good way to improve memory is by getting plenty of sleep. Recent research shows that sleep actually helps process memories and speed up learning. During sleep, the brain strengthens the synapses between the nerve cells that form memories.

Sleep is an unavoidable, time-consuming event that occupies about one-third of a human's life. Even though everyone sleeps, not every person needs the same amount of sleep. Most adults generally sleep eight hours a night, although a few function on as little as one or two hours of sleep, while others require ten or twelve. Children sleep more than adults, and babies may sleep sixteen out of every twenty-four hours.

Early scientists were interested in the phenomenon of sleep and speculated as to its cause. Aristotle had an interesting theory. He wrote that the digestion of food produces warm vapors that rise from the stomach and collect in the head. In the brain, these vapors cool and condense, then flow downward to the heart. He reasoned that cooling of the heart, which he considered to be the body's sensory center, caused sleep.

The Biological Clock

It was not until the early twentieth century that scientists began to realize that sleep was an important, active event. Before this time, it was generally believed that sleep was simply a dormant period, a time of rest caused by fatigue or lack of stimulation. Research has shown that this is not true. Sleep is initiated and maintained by specific areas within the brain.

It is now known that periods of sleep and wakefulness in many living things are regulated by a biological clock. In humans, this clock is a tiny mass of neurons in the brain's hypothalamus. The clock sets wake-up and sleep periods. A person's biological clock is controlled by the amount of sunlight entering the eye and traveling to the brain. Light activates the tiny pineal gland, which makes the sleep-inducing brain chemical called melatonin. Production of melatonin stops during daylight hours.

Brain Waves

Research on the brain and sleep was accelerated by the invention in 1929 of the electroencephalograph, which makes it possible to analyze brain activity. An electroencephalograph creates a picture called an electroencephalogram, or EEG, which is a unique view of a person's brain activity. EEGs, which can show changes in the brain's level of activity, have proved useful in studying different levels of alertness and have been used extensively in the study of sleep.

Most EEGs on sleeping subjects are recorded in sleep labs, special facilities equipped with electroencephalography units for the investigators and beds for the subjects. In these experiments, a researcher attaches to a subject's head electrodes that detect electrical activity in the brain.

EEGs show that the amount of brain electrical activity decreases as a person moves from wakefulness to sleep. The

EEG electrodes allow scientists to monitor brain activity during sleep. The large amount of data collected in one night is fed directly to a computer for analysis.

brain of an alert person produces rapid brain waves. As a person relaxes and begins to fall asleep, brain waves slow down. As sleep deepens, brain waves continue to slow.

As the brain moves into a period of sleep, it affects the rest of the body. A person who is awake unconsciously depends on large muscles to provide strength and balance for standing, sitting, and moving. Sometimes, just at the point of drifting off to sleep, muscles that had been relaxing contract suddenly and cause a jumping movement called a hypnic jerk. This jolt, which is often preceded by the sensation of falling, can be so startling that it wakes the sleeper. Researchers have no explanation for it. Researchers also have been unable to pinpoint from EEGs the exact moment of falling asleep.

Stages of Sleep

By studying EEGs, muscle tone, and other indicators of sleep, researchers have found that sleep is an active event that follows a regular cycle each night. Sleep can be divided into different levels or stages. As the sleeper travels through these stages, the level of brain activity goes through a roller-coaster series of changes.

The relaxed period of drifting off to sleep is called stage 1. During this time, brain waves are only slightly less frequent than they are when the brain is alert. Breathing becomes regular and heart rate begins to slow. The eyes occasionally roll back in the head. This vertical eye movement can be easily seen in babies because they sleep with their eyes half open. Their irises and pupils seem to disappear for a short time, revealing only the whites of the eyes. Once asleep, these eye movements stop.

As sleep deepens, the sleeper moves into the phase called stage 2. Brain waves shift to a slower frequency, but the sleeper can still be awakened easily. Muscles continue to relax, and breathing and heart rates slow even more. In stage 3, the frequency of brain waves continues to slow, and awakening is more difficult.

By stage 4, brain waves have reached their slowest rate and awakening is difficult. At this stage, muscles are completely relaxed, and both heart and breathing rates are slow and regular. A person awakened from deep sleep does not adjust immediately and may feel confused and groggy for a few minutes. People who walk in their sleep, experience night terrors, or wet the bed are in deep sleep and do not realize what is happening at the time of these acts.

Something New

After ten to fifteen minutes at the deepest level, the sleeper begins to move back up the stages of sleep. First, the sleeper ascends to stage 3, then a few minutes later moves to stage 2. However, instead of reentering stage 1, as one might expect, the sleeper moves into an entirely different

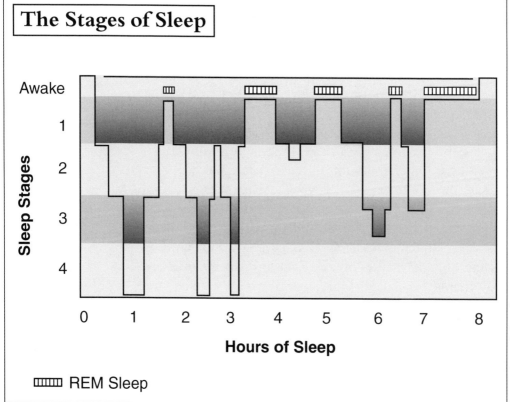

The Stages of Sleep

Sleep Stages

Awake
1
2
3
4

0 1 2 3 4 5 6 7 8

Hours of Sleep

▥▥▥▥ REM Sleep

phase. Breathing becomes more rapid and irregular, heart rate increases, blood pressure rises, and the eyes begin to move quickly from side to side. Brain waves return to alert levels, a change that seems to indicate a light stage of sleep. However, the sleeper is not in a light stage, and awakening is not easy. This turn of events begins a stage described as rapid eye movement, or REM, sleep. Named for the characteristic motion of the eyes, REM sleep is an active period that often involves dreaming.

Characteristics of REM Sleep

During stages 1 through 4, skeletal muscles, the muscles responsible for movement, are relaxed. However, in the REM sleep, skeletal muscle tone changes dramatically. All skeletal muscles become completely paralyzed. This radical adjustment in muscle tone is controlled by the brain. When a person is awake, electrical impulses generated by areas of the brain that control muscle movements travel down the spine and out to the individual muscles, controlling their behavior. However, in REM sleep, these impulses are inhibited and the muscles do not receive information from the brain. Consequently, the muscles are not able to contract. The only muscles not affected by this inhibition center are those that control movements of the eyes.

One theory suggests that the function of muscle inactivation during REM sleep is to prevent the sleeper from acting out dreams. Studies on cats seem to offer confirmation of this idea. In a series of experiments, researchers severed the nerve cells that inhibit muscle movement in the brains of cats. When these animals entered REM sleep, they jumped around their cages, hissing, swatting, or running as if in combat with a dream-generated foe.

The initial REM period in a night's sleep is usually short, only five to ten minutes. After the first REM stage, the sleeper drifts back down through stages 2, 3, and 4. After ten or fifteen minutes in stage 4, the sleeper moves back up through stages 3 and 2 and reenters the REM phase, this time for twelve to fifteen minutes. This pattern of drifting through sleep phases is repeated several times during the night, and with each succeeding sleep cycle, the REM stages last longer. A complete sleep cycle lasts about ninety minutes, and the number of cycles that one experiences in a night depends on the length of the sleep period. It is not unusual for a person to cycle through the REM stage three or four times, experiencing as many as a dozen dreams in one night.

Very hot or cold sleeping environments can interfere with REM sleep because the temperature-controlling part of the brain is not active during this stage of sleep. Interestingly, if REM sleep is interrupted or shortened one night, the body will make up for it the next. Instead of slowly moving through each stage of sleep, the REM-deprived sleeper slips directly into REM sleep and stays in that stage longer than usual.

Dreams

Most dreams occur during REM sleep. One of the earliest methods that sleep researchers used to learn about dreams was to wake up sleeping subjects during their REM sleep. When awakened from REM sleep, 80 percent of the subjects could remember a few minutes of their dreams. Researchers also found that deep sleepers were less likely to remember their dreams than light sleepers were. Some subjects could never remember their dreams, no matter when they were awakened.

Dreams occupy about two hours of each sleep period. They are not limited to REM sleep, but can occur in all stages. However, REM dreams are usually more vivid and detailed than dreams in other periods. People often dream about everyday experiences from the previous week, but memories from the distant past also can form the basis of dramatic or puzzling dream sequences.

No one really knows the function of dreams in any stage of sleep, but research from several different labs provides clues. Because the brain is very active during dreaming, some scientists suggest that dreams play a role in keeping the nervous system in good working order. Other research implies that since dreams often review recent experiences, they help the brain sort through memories and solve problems. These theories are not mutually exclusive; dreams may be critical in several physiological functions.

Deep Sleep and Lack of Sleep

All stages of sleep serve restorative functions. Whereas research suggests that REM, or dream sleep, has a function in keeping the brain healthy, deep sleep seems to play a role in keeping the body healthy. Deep sleep is the time when the body is not obliged to devote energy to complex physical activities and can focus on healing and repairing damage from the activities of the day. During deep sleep, cell production is accelerated and growth hormone is produced. Without this essential chemical, children would never increase in size, and tissues could not be repaired.

Without adequate sleep, the body does not function at its best. In situations where sleep is prevented for a long period of time, the body ceases to function altogether. Experiments show that animals who are deprived of sleep for seven to ten days develop sores on their body and die. From this research, scientists have discovered a paradox; just as REM sleep seems to affect the activity of the brain cells that regulate body temperature, prolonged lack of sleep produces a similar effect. Sleep-deprived animals are unable to maintain stable body temperature and die of heat loss. The sores that form before their death may be the result of infections due to malfunctioning immune systems.

Resting and Remembering

When an important decision is to be made, people often choose to "sleep on it." For years it has been suspected that sleep plays a role in several higher brain functions

Growth hormone is produced during deep sleep. Without this vital chemical, children would never increase in size.

such as learning and memory. New research showing that sleep is an active process has led to the conclusion that sleep is just as important as any other brain function. People deprived of sleep for short periods feel tired and irritable, are prone to making mistakes, and are less creative than usual. To function at its best, the human body must have plenty of sleep.

All types of scientific research have contributed to understanding memory and sleep. Animal studies have provided valuable evidence about the functions of nervous systems. With the advent of EEGs, scientists found a method of studying brain activity in people. Similarly, the movement of electrical activity through the brain can be followed by means of magnetic resonance and other imaging techniques.

Scientists have a lot to learn about how the brain processes and saves information. Sleeping and dreaming may be periods when the brain assimilates information it has taken in during the day. Dreaming provides an opportunity for the brain to review experiences and store some of them in memory.

Assault on the Body's Communication System

4

The central and peripheral nervous systems control the body. Therefore, they are in charge of a variety of body functions ranging from heart rate to bladder control and from memory to anger. For this reason, conditions that damage the nervous system produce a wide range of symptoms. Pain, loss of sensation, mental confusion, seizures, paralysis, and inability to speak are just a few of the thousands of problems that can result.

Some of the factors that can compromise or damage the human nervous system include assault by infectious agents, trauma sustained by injury, degenerative disease processes, vascular disorders, development of tumors, and exposure to toxic chemicals.

Swollen Tissue in the Brain

Because it is guarded by the bony skull, strong membranes, and an efficient blood-brain barrier, the central nervous system is better protected from infection than other body systems. However, it is not impossible for pathogens, or disease-causing microorganisms, to breach the body's security systems. When this happens, serious infections can result.

Meningitis, the inflammation of the coverings (meninges) of the brain and spinal cord, is a dangerous condition that can be caused by either bacteria or viruses. These pathogens gain entry to the nervous system from the bloodstream, through direct penetration from surgery or injury, or from infected sinus cavities.

Bacterial meningitis is more common than viral meningitis. Children between the ages of one month and two years are the group most susceptible to developing this condition. However, adults who have compromised immune systems and those with chronic respiratory infections can also develop meningitis.

One of the cardinal symptoms of meningitis is stiffness in the neck, which can be so severe that it prevents a person from lowering their chin to the chest. However, in children younger than one year of age, the first symptoms may be fever, sore throat, headache, or vomiting. Confusion and sleepiness may appear within twenty-four hours after a person is infected with a pathogen that causes meningitis. Swelling of brain tissue due to infection can interfere with normal blood flow in

Bacteria causing meningitis typically grow in pairs or clumps. The deadly disease infects brain tissue, causing it to swell.

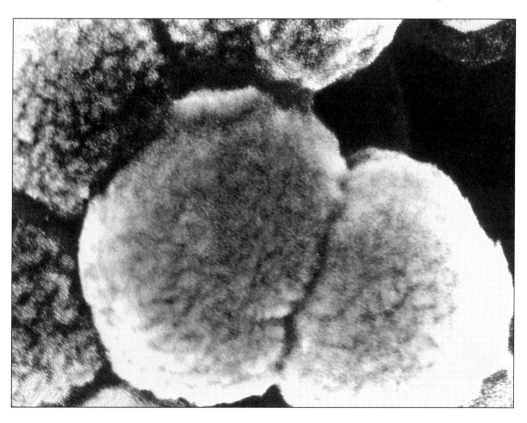

the brain, causing seizures and stroke. Without prompt medical intervention, coma and death may follow.

One of the keys to successful treatment of meningitis is quick diagnosis of the disease. To confirm an identification of meningitis, physicians must remove a sample of cerebrospinal fluid from the fluid-filled space surrounding the spinal column. Part of this sample is immediately observed under the microscope to check for the presence of pathogens. The remaining portion of the sample is sent to the lab so that any organisms extracted can be cultured, or grown in small flasks or petri dishes. Culturing a pathogen enables a physician to confirm its identity and test the effectiveness of different medications against it.

Since meningitis can be fatal in a very short time, doctors do not wait for lab results and often start patients on a combination of antibiotics as soon as microscopic examination of cerebrospinal fluid has revealed pathogens. After the specific disease-causing pathogen has been identified, medication can be adjusted if necessary. Since viruses cannot be killed with antibiotics, viral meningitis is primarily treated with medications and techniques that help manage the symptoms.

If treatment for meningitis is started quickly, chances of survival are 90 percent. Even though most people recover fully, an unfortunate few develop seizures or suffer some form of permanent brain damage. There is a vaccine available that protects against the most common causes of meningitis. However, since few people contract meningitis and because all vaccines carry a risk of side effects, its use is recommended only in case of an epidemic or for people who live in closed populations, like a military base, where contagious diseases are easily spread.

Rabies

Rabies is another serious infection of the nervous system. People can get this disease if they are bitten by infected warm-blooded animals, such as raccoons, foxes, bats, cats, and dogs. Rabies is caused by a virus that is transmitted

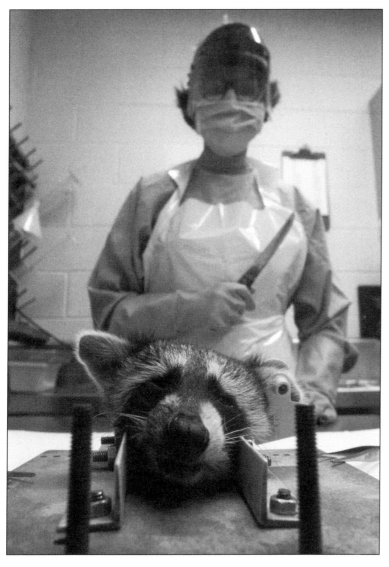

To test this raccoon for rabies, a researcher prepares to remove some of the animal's brain tissue.

through the saliva of an infected animal. When introduced to the body through a wound, the virus migrates to the nearest nerves, then travels along the nervous system to the spinal cord and brain. In the brain the virus multiplies, destroying brain tissue. It reaches the salivary glands and saliva through nerves that connect the brain to the mouth. The speed at which the virus gets to a victim's brain depends on the distance of the wound from the brain. Neck and face wounds produce symptoms quicker than wounds to the leg or foot.

Signs of infection appear within forty to sixty days after the virus has entered the victim's body. Initial symptoms may be feelings of depression or restlessness that eventually evolve into uncontrollable excitement. As the disease progresses, the victim suffers fever and pain. Paralysis may begin in the legs and progress up through the body. Infected animals and people secrete large amounts of sticky saliva. Painful spasms of the throat and voice box make it impossible to drink. Infection with rabies is also called hydrophobia, a name that means "fear of water."

People who suspect they have been bitten by a rabid animal are advised to get treatment immediately. If treatment is delayed, the virus may have time to reach the brain, a circumstance that makes death inevitable. Treatment begins with a thorough cleaning of the wound. People who have been previously vaccinated against rabies are given an injection of rabies immunoglobulin, which consists of pathogen-destroying proteins. Victims who have not been vaccinated against rabies receive immunoglobulin as well as injections of rabies vaccine on the day of exposure, and again on days three, seven, fourteen, and twenty-eight. Vaccines contain a deactivated form of the rabies virus that stimulates the body to make antibodies that can destroy the virus before it reaches the brain.

The best way to manage rabies is through prevention. Public health officials and humane societies advise pet owners to have their animals vaccinated yearly to protect them from infection by unvaccinated or wild animals. To be safe, people are advised to avoid handling any wild animals. One early sign of rabies infection in animals is a change of temperament; tame animals become aggressive and wild animals seem tame or friendly. As the disease advances, the animal behaves in a confused and disoriented manner, and thick ropes of saliva collect around the mouth.

Tetanus

Another infectious agent that enters the body through a wound is *Clostridium tetani,* the bacterium that causes tetanus. Tetanus, commonly called lockjaw, is a disease of the nervous system that can be fatal. Tetanus bacteria, which live in the soil and in animal manure, enter the body through punctures in the skin of the foot or elsewhere. People who have burns or other wounds are especially at risk, as well as those who take drugs by injection.

Once inside the body, tetanus bacteria reproduce and release destructive toxins. Symptoms may appear as early as three days or as late as three weeks after infection. Although the symptoms of tetanus can vary from one individual to another, one of the classic signs is stiffness of the jaw muscle—

A young boy receives a tetanus vaccine. The disease attacks the nervous system and, if left untreated, can result in death.

hence the term *lockjaw.* This is usually followed by stiffness of the neck, difficulty in swallowing, rigidity of abdominal muscles, spasms, fever, and sweating. Death may occur if spasms of the respiratory muscles interfere with breathing. In less severe cases, symptoms are limited to the muscles near the site of injury.

Doctors usually base a diagnosis of tetanus on a patient's description of their symptoms. Treatment begins with a thorough cleaning of the wound and removal of any dead tissue that can promote bacterial growth. Injections of tetanus immunoglobulins are given, because these protein substances can destroy the tetanus toxin. If a patient has not had a tetanus vaccination within the last ten years, one or more injections of vaccine will be administered. Antibiotics are given to stop further growth of the bacteria. The best way to deal with tetanus is to prevent it.

In the United States, diphtheria, tetanus, and pertussis, or DTP, vaccine is mandated for children to protect them from disease. Booster immunizations are recommended every ten years.

Neurological Breakdown: Alzheimer's Disease

Not all neurological diseases can be attributed to infectious agents. There are several degenerative brain diseases that may have multiple triggering mechanisms. Alzheimer's disease is one of these. The exact cause of Alzheimer's disease is not known, but scientists speculate that viruses, metallic toxins, genetic factors, and abnormal neurotransmitters may all play a role. No matter what the cause, this disease has two devastating effects: It damages neurons in specific parts of the brain, and it reduces production of acetylcholine, a neurotransmitter.

Destruction of brain tissue by Alzheimer's disease takes place over a period of years. Former president Ronald Reagan announced in 1994 that he had Alzheimer's disease, but the public had long before noticed that Reagan was having difficulties with his memory. The symptoms of Alzheimer's disease affect people in stages. In the first stage, victims misplace objects and forget names. In the next stage, forgetfulness gives way to confusion, and the person is no longer able to perform quality work. In later stages, the patient may act aggressively, feel anxious, and have trouble sleeping. Some patients wander away from their homes and are unable to find their way back because they cannot orient themselves. In the last stages of Alzheimer's disease, the person may become completely incapacitated, losing the ability to walk and talk. Death is caused by loss of nerve cells in the brain, and it usually occurs from five to fifteen years after the onset.

A Difficult Diagnosis

Alzheimer's disease is not easy to diagnose because there is no test of blood or other body fluid that will reveal its presence. Thus, a variety of medical tests are often performed

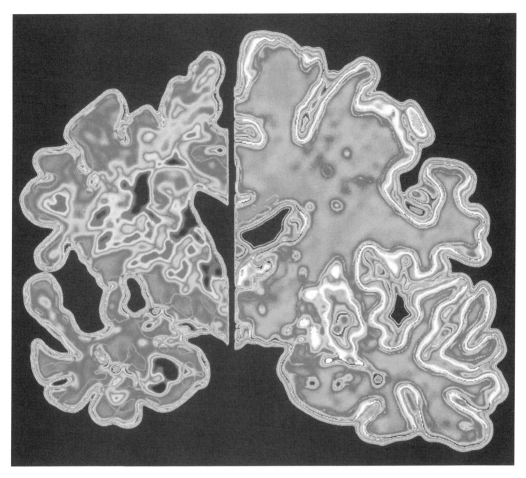

to eliminate the possibility that other diseases are responsible for the symptoms. In fact, the only way to verify a diagnosis of Alzheimer's is by autopsy, after the patient dies. The first case of the disease was described in 1906 by Alois Alzheimer, a German neurologist. A patient of his had been inexplicably confused prior to her death, and Alzheimer ordered an autopsy. When he examined tissue from her brain under the microscope he saw neurons clumped together, which he called tangles, and accumulated clusters of proteins, which he called plaques. Alzheimer theorized that the presence of these plaques interfered with proper neuron function and prevented normal cellular communication.

A computer image shows the brain of an Alzheimer's patient (left) and a normal brain. The Alzheimer's brain shows evidence of tissue destruction.

There is no cure for Alzheimer's disease, but there are medications to slow the progression of the disease and ease the symptoms. Two drugs that were approved by the U.S. Food and Drug Administration (FDA) are presently being used to increase the levels of the neurotransmitter, acetylcholine, in the brain. This helps to slow memory loss. There are several other drugs awaiting FDA approval.

Shaking Palsy

Parkinson's disease, like Alzheimer's disease, is a degenerative brain disorder. Sometimes referred to as shaking palsy, Parkinson's disease causes uncontrollable body tremors. In the early stages, tremors may be mild, but over time the shaking movements become more pronounced. The hands, lips, and legs are usually the areas of the body that suffer the most tremors. Other symptoms include stiff limbs, slow movements, loss of facial expression, and the tendency to remain in one position for long periods of time. Even though the disease interferes with a person's quality of life, it does not usually lead to a premature death.

Scientists have determined that the cause of Parkinson's disease is an inadequate supply of dopamine, a neurotransmitter. This chemical is vital to the transmission of nerve impulses to the region of the brain that controls smooth, rapid movements of muscles. In the part of the cerebrum called the basal ganglia, the neurotransmitters dopamine and acetylcholine work together to relay accurate messages to each other. When dopamine levels are low, the balance of the two essential chemicals is disrupted and messages cannot be relayed to the center of the brain that controls movement.

Uncontrollable shaking of the hands is usually the first symptom that prompts a person to seek help. Physicians often diagnose the disease after a physical exam and medical history. Imaging techniques can be used to rule out the possibility of other neurological disorders.

There is no cure for Parkinson's disease, but certain drugs can alleviate some of the symptoms. A common medication prescribed for Parkinson's disease is L-dopa, a compound that is converted into dopamine in the patient's body. The diagnosis of Parkinson's is confirmed if symptoms subside after administration of L-dopa has raised dopamine levels. Scientists are experimenting with a procedure to transplant new dopamine-producing tissue into the brain of Parkinson's patients.

Scientists are investigating risk factors that make one person more prone to developing this disease than others. They know, for example, that Parkinsonism can result when other degenerative diseases, drugs, or toxins interfere with

Actor Michael J. Fox has Parkinson's disease. The condition causes uncontrolled body tremors that increase in intensity over time.

the production of dopamine. The illegal street drug known as N–MPTP can produce Parkinson's disease. It is believed that repeated head trauma (such as that received in the sport of boxing) can accelerate the onset of Parkinson's.

Head Trauma and Electrical Brain Storms

Head trauma is the leading cause of accidental death in the United States. Despite the protection provided by the shock-absorbing cerebrospinal fluid, a blow to the head can cause the brain to ricochet off the inside of the skull. Even slight injury to the brain can produce a concussion, a condition that can cause a temporary loss of consciousness and leave a person dizzy, confused, or abnormally sleepy. A more serious condition, a contusion, results when a blow to the head seriously damages tissue in the brain. Contusions often accompany serious head wounds and produce a variety of symptoms depending on severity.

Head injuries can trigger a group of symptoms called epilepsy. The word *epilepsy* means "to seize or hold." Victims of epilepsy experience repeated seizures, episodes that are sometimes described as electrical storms in the brain. Seizures result when neurons in the brain misfire, creating abnormal electrical impulses that cause involuntary body movements and muscle spasms.

Head injuries are not the only causes of epileptic seizures. They can also be caused by brain tumors, strokes, bacterial infections, and blockages in arteries leading to the brain. A few types of epilepsy are inherited. About 50 percent to 70 percent of epilepsy cases are described as idiopathic because they have no known cause.

The EEG records of people with epilepsy indicate unusually high levels of electrical activity. Imaging techniques can be used to see if brain tissue has been damaged by the seizures. Epilepsy cannot be cured, but sometimes it can be controlled with drugs called anticonvulsants, which reduce the abnormal firing of neurons in the brain. If these drugs are ineffective, damaged parts of the brain can be removed.

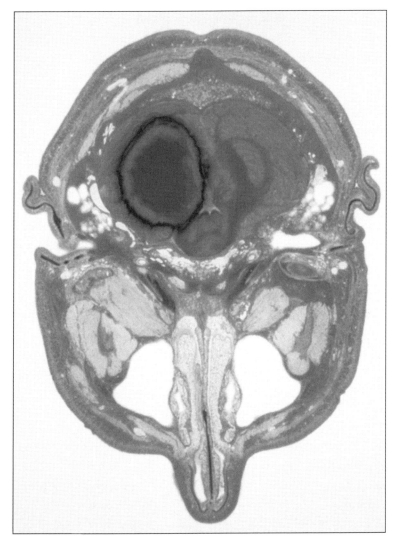

A digital illustration reveals a cerebral hemorrhage (dark, circular area) caused by a stroke.

Cerebrovascular Accidents

A stroke, one of the most common disorders of the nervous system, can lead to epileptic seizures and other serious conditions. Statistics show that strokes are the cause of more neurological damage than any other disease in the United States, where someone suffers a stroke every sixty seconds.

Physicians sometimes refer to strokes as cerebrovascular accidents. A stroke results when an artery carrying oxygen-rich blood to the brain is obstructed or ruptured. Strokes can be caused by blood clots in the arteries servicing the brain or by development of hemorrhages in these arteries. In either case, oxygen is prevented from traveling to its destination. If this situation is not quickly corrected, cells of the brain become oxygen-starved and are consequently damaged or destroyed. A patient who survives a stroke may lose function in the parts of the body that should be controlled by the damaged nerves in the brain.

The most common causes of strokes are blood clots that develop inside of arteries leading to the brain. As a clot thickens over time, it blocks more and more of the blood vessel. Prior to complete obstruction, a person may develop symptoms such as dizziness, confusion, numbness or paralysis on one side of the body, visual disturbances, loss of balance, headaches, fainting, or difficulty speaking. Once a blood vessel traveling to the brain is completely blocked, loss of consciousness can occur and death may quickly follow. Not all strokes are fatal; their severity depends on the size of the vessel affected. Medication is available that can dissolve a blood clot if it is administered within three hours of symptoms of a stroke.

The site and extent of brain damage determines the outcome for the stroke victim. Patients who survive a stroke often have difficulty speaking. Speech can return over time, sometimes after therapy. Many stroke victims are left with other types of physical disabilities, depending on the group of motor neurons that were damaged during the stroke. Paralysis can be either temporary or permanent in body parts controlled by these motor neurons.

The incidence of stroke is more prevalent in certain groups of people. Two-thirds of all stroke victims are over age sixty-five. Men are more likely to have a stroke than women, and African Americans suffer more strokes than any other ethnic group. A person's chances of having a stroke also increase if they are diabetic or have high blood pressure, high cholesterol, or heart disease. Smoking, drinking alcohol, obesity, and sedentary lifestyle are also risk factors for strokes.

People who have symptoms of a stroke are advised to seek medical help immediately. Imaging tests, ultrasounds, and nuclear imaging techniques can be employed to locate blocked cerebral arteries. If blockages are discovered, doctors may suggest an operation called an endarterectomy. This is a common surgical procedure that removes the thickened area that is creating the blockage inside the blood vessel.

Abnormal Growths in the Brain

Strokes are not the only nervous system disorder that can require surgery. A brain tumor can be just as dangerous as a stroke. A brain tumor is a cluster of abnormal cells that grow in the brain. It can be cancerous (malignant) or noncancerous

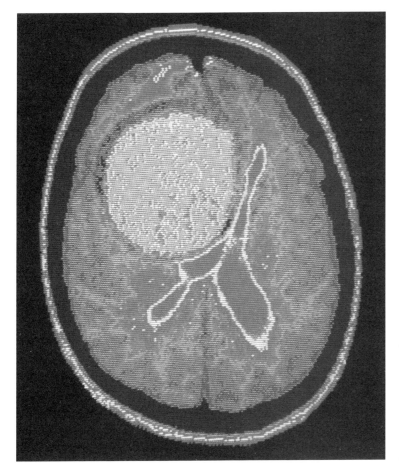

A CT scan shows a large brain tumor (light-colored mass at center). Such tumors may be benign or malignant and are often surgically removed.

(benign). Cancerous tumors that develop in the brain are called primary tumors. However, most cancerous brain tumors begin life elsewhere in the body, then migrate to the brain. The lungs, breast, prostate, or colon are common sites of origin for cancers that can spread to the brain.

The symptoms of brain tumors vary from person to person. As a tumor grows, it puts pressure on the brain, causing symptoms such as headaches, blurred vision, vomiting, and mental confusion. Speech and motor skills can be affected if the tumor damages or destroys the part of the brain controlling those functions. Doctors generally rely on imaging technologies such as MRI to diagnose a tumor.

Surgery is often the recommended treatment for brain tumors. Because they usually have well-defined borders, many benign tumors can be removed by skilled surgeons. Malignant tumors are harder to remove because the margins of a cancerous tumor are not well defined. Consequently, surgeons sometimes cut away only enough of the tumor to relieve pressure in the skull, trying to leave intact as much delicate brain tissue as possible. Radiation and chemotherapies are often used to destroy the remaining cancer cells. Despite all these treatments, sometimes the growth of a cancerous tumor may prove to be unstoppable, causing death.

Scientists are not sure why brain tumors develop, but several factors seem to contribute to their formation. Both adults and children can fall victim to tumors due to genetic abnormalities, errors in fetal development, exposure to radiation, viral infections, injuries, malfunctions in the immune system, or hormonal abnormalities.

Interfering with Connections

Synapses, the junction between neurons and other cells, and neurotransmitters, the chemicals that carry messages across synapses, must be functioning correctly for the nervous system to do its job. Any condition that alters the release or uptake of neurotransmitters compromises the

nervous system's ability to function. Two common drugs, tobacco and alcohol, do just that.

A gruesome illustration depicts the deadly result of tobacco use. Nicotine stimulates the brain's neurotransmitters, causing a sense of well-being.

Tobacco

People have smoked, chewed, and otherwise used tobacco for thousands of years. The tobacco plant contains nicotine, a potent natural chemical that disturbs normal functions of the nervous system. Nicotine stimulates the body through its effects on neurotransmitters in the brain. As a consequence, heart and respiratory rates increase, and blood pressure escalates.

After traveling the full length of a neuron, an electrical impulse reaches the synapse, where it causes the release of a neurotransmitter. This chemical travels across the synapse and binds with the postsynaptic cell. The ability of a neurotransmitter to bind with receptors at the postsynaptic site is a critical factor in stimulating the next cell.

Just like a neurotransmitter, nicotine has the ability to bind with receptors on postsynaptic nerves. Normally, the regulatory system of the human body controls the amount of neurotransmitters that are produced, preventing inappropriate stimulation of nerves. However, the body cannot regulate levels of nicotine taken in through smoking. Consequently, smoking can flood many areas of the brain with nicotine, overstimulating neurons and giving the body an unnatural surge of energy.

Almost everyone who uses tobacco is aware of its negative consequences, yet people continue to use the drug. Nicotine is a difficult chemical to give up for two reasons. It causes the release of neurotransmitters in the reward pathways, those parts of the brain that produce a pleasant feeling when they are stimulated. Nicotine also increases the levels of a group of natural chemicals, endorphins. Like the reward pathway, endorphins give the body a feeling of peace and well-being.

Alcohol

Alcohol is another commonly used chemical that has detrimental effects on the nervous system. Alcoholic beverages are made from the distillation of certain fruits or grains. When drinks are consumed, the alcohol interferes with communication between nerve cells and other types of cells. One way it does this is by boosting the effects of the neurotransmitter GABA, whose job is to inhibit transmission of nerve impulses. By enhancing an inhibitor and thus hindering the travel of impulses across synapses, alcohol makes many body functions slow down. Alcohol also reduces the levels of glutamine, a neurotransmitter that excites or stimulates nerves. Thus, by decreasing the amount of stimulation the nerves receive, alcohol slows the body in another way.

Alcohol affects all areas of the brain, but it gets to some areas before others. The order in which it interferes with brain function is similar to the order in which brain structures are arranged in the skull. First, alcohol slows the cerebral cortex, then the limbic system, cerebellum, hypothalamus, and finally the brain stem. When alcohol reaches the cerebral cortex, it has several effects. It prevents the functioning of areas that curb some behaviors, causing the person drinking alcohol to lose inhibitions that normally govern interactions with other people. Alcohol also raises the level of pain that a person can tolerate, and it slows down the ability to process sensory information, so the drinker responds to new information very slowly.

Once alcohol reaches the limbic system, it begins to increase emotional feelings such as anger or fear, and it contributes to memory loss. When it reaches the cerebellum it interferes with muscle movement and balance, causing lack of balance and coordination. These effects on the cerebellum lead to a stage that some people describe as "falling down drunk." Alcohol slows down the areas of hypothalamus in command of sexual performance, but not the parts that control sexual excitement. It also inhibits production of the hormone that directs the kidneys to return water to the body. Consequently, kidneys produce more urine.

The brain stem regulates breathing, heart rate, and consciousness. Therefore, when alcohol reaches this area, it makes a person feel sleepy. Very high quantities of alcohol can cause loss of consciousness. Extremely high levels of alcohol in the blood can suppress breathing altogether, causing death.

Deadly Consequences

Centuries ago, early physicians had little understanding of disorders of the brain. Evil spirits were blamed for a variety of disorders ranging from epilepsy to dementia. At one time, physicians treated their patients for these conditions by drilling holes in their heads to let the spirits escape.

Today, physicians and scientists understand how damage to the nervous system can produce a variety of symptoms. The symptoms experienced by an individual depend on the portion of the brain or nervous system affected as well as the causes. Infectious agents such as bacteria and viruses can bring about the inflammatory diseases of meningitis, rabies, and tetanus. Alzheimer's disease and

Parkinson's disease are types of degenerative brain disorders that can disrupt parts of the body controlled by the nervous system. Accidents such as head injuries can cause concussions and contusions that can lead to epileptic seizures or death. Nervous-system disorders, such as strokes, are caused by disruptions in the vascular system that feeds oxygen to the brain. Brain tumors, cancerous and noncancerous, are both difficult to understand and to treat. Even common drugs like nicotine and alcohol interfere with the brain's ability to function normally. Understanding the agents and mechanisms causing these conditions helps scientists search for new and better ways to treat disorders of the brain and nervous system.

5 Probing and Exploring the Nervous System

People who suffer from disorders that affect the brain, spinal cord, or peripheral nerves need special medical attention. The branch of medicine that deals with the nervous system is neurology, and doctors who specialize in the diagnosis and treatment of its disorders are neurologists. Patients are often referred to neurologists by their general practitioners.

To help patients, a neurologist must fully understand their problems. The first step in solving a neurological mystery is to review the patient's medical history and identify current symptoms. A medical assessment is generally the next step. This exam consists of a series of simple tests that evaluate all body systems but concentrate specifically on the nervous system. If more information is needed, the doctor may order one or more detailed tests. The results of these explorations help establish proper treatment.

A Doctor's First Clue

When conducting neurological physical exams, physicians follow a routine that allows them systematically to access the function of each part of the nervous system. Several simple tests provide useful information on the condition of cranial nerves, motor neurons, sensory neurons, reflexes, coordination, the autonomic nervous system, and blood flow to the brain.

The twelve pairs of cranial nerves connect directly to the brain, and it is important to determine if one of them is damaged. The ability to smell, see, hear, and swallow are some of the functions evaluated during the cranial nerve testing. Motor neurons allow the muscles to move properly. The neurologist visually looks for evidence of muscle loss and performs strength tests in which a patient is asked to push or pull against a resistance. Sensory neurons carry information to the brain about pressure, temperature, and pain. Doctors test for proper functioning of sensory neurons by checking to see if the patient can distinguish between the touch of sharp and dull objects.

One neurological experiment that is familiar to many people is the knee-jerk reflex test. It evaluates a person's ability to respond to a stimulus. This test is conducted while a patient sits on a high table with the feet not touching the floor. The doctor taps a tendon below the kneecap with a small rubber hammer. The reaction of a knee jerk shows that all of the nerves between the tendon and the spinal cord as well as those that connect the spinal cord to the leg muscle are functioning properly.

The ability of the brain and nervous system to maintain proper stance and gait are evaluated by asking a patient to stand still with arms outstretched and eyes closed, then walk a few steps. Since a malfunction of the autonomic nervous system can cause blood pressure to drop upon standing, doctors monitor difference in blood pressure between sitting and standing. Neurologists check proper blood flow to the brain by placing a stethoscope directly over the arteries of the neck. If the obstructions have caused the arteries to narrow, blood forced through a narrowed opening produces abnormal sounds.

After the physical exam, doctors may order more sophisticated tests to clarify what is going on inside each patient's nervous system. These tests help doctors form a diagnosis.

A Look Inside the Body

Traditional X rays of the spine and skull are the simplest imaging procedures. The presence of tumors or bone abnormalities of the skull and spinal cord can often be de-

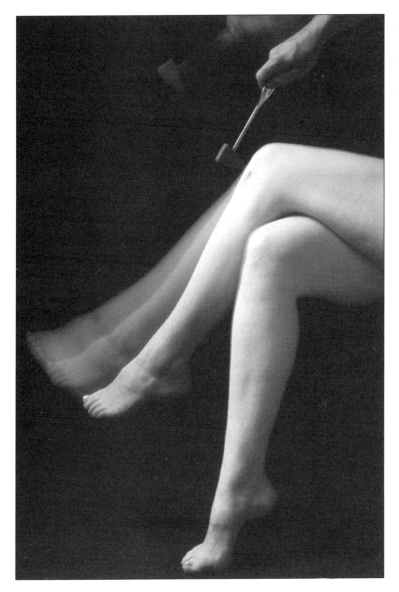

A doctor taps the tendon below a patient's knee, triggering the knee-jerk reflex. The test demonstrates proper nerve function.

tected by examination of the X-ray films. When their flow is not blocked, X rays travel through the body and strike a photographic plate on the opposite side. These rays expose the photographic film, creating dark areas. However, X rays that are absorbed by dense material in the body, like tumors, fluid, or bone, produce a white shadow on the film.

If a physician needs to see more detail than can be provided by a simple X ray, a contrast medium may be used. A contrast medium is a chemical dye that is injected into a patient's body to enhance the image produced on the X ray. The dye, often iodine, is very dense. Like bone, it absorbs the X rays and produces a white image on the film corresponding to the location of the dye. Since some patients are subject to allergic reactions to the contrast medium, medical personnel question patients prior to testing to determine if they have an allergy to iodine.

Enhancing the Look

X rays with contrast media are helpful when examining the arteries that provide blood to the brain. Use of dye in these specific arteries is called cerebral angiography. In this procedure, dye is injected into the arteries through a thin tube called a catheter. As the dye streams through the arteries, its progress is tracked by a video camera. Once injected, the dye flows through the cerebral arteries and outlines their shapes. It creates a white area on X-ray film that helps physicians find narrow sections, blockages, or bulges in the arteries. This test helps doctors to evaluate a patient's risk for stroke or for aneurysm, a weak place in a blood vessel.

If a spinal cord disorder is suspected, the physician may order X rays with contrast media for the spinal cord. The resulting images are called myelograms, and they can show doctors if any nerves are being compressed near the spinal cord.

A Specialized Look

Traditional X rays are often used to get the first view of the inside of a patient's body. Sometimes, however, this century-old technique cannot provide enough information about the area being explored. In recent years, new technologies have been developed to provide details about the interior of the body.

Brain scans are a group of imaging techniques that were developed to combine images taken from several different angles into one single picture of the brain. They can be performed by either computerized axial tomography, so-called CT scans, or by MRIs. Instead of sending one wide beam of energy through a patient, as in a traditional X ray, a CT scan transmits numerous narrow X rays through the brain. A camera rotates around the patient's head, recording

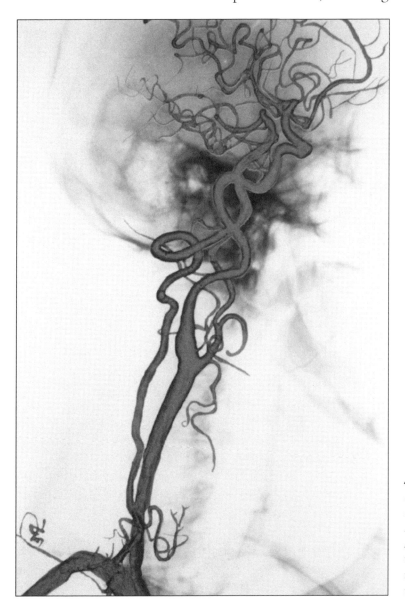

A brain angiogram reveals the arteries in the head and neck. The arteries have been injected with a chemical dye to enhance their visibility.

information and sending it directly to a computer. As in traditional X rays, some body structures absorb the rays while others allow them to pass through to the film. A CT scan produces a series of cross-sectional images that look like slices of the brain. Doctors called radiologists, who interpret the scans, can discern abnormalities that are hazy or invisible on traditional X rays. CT scans, like traditional X rays, can be performed using contrast media dye to enhance images of blood vessels.

In MRIs, computer analysis of the energy emitted by molecules within the brain results in images of the brain tissue. During an MRI session, the patient's head is placed inside a device that emits strong magnetic energy. Normal and abnormal tissues in the brain respond by emitting different amounts of energy, and these responses are converted to electrical signals. Computers collect the signals and output them as visual images that doctors can view. Inspection of MRIs helps physicians to diagnose tumors, infections, and other nervous-system abnormalities. The images can also be used to reveal the patterns of blood flow through arteries in the neck and through the base of the brain. MRIs do not involve the use of radiation, but the process by which they are made is more expensive and time-consuming than X-ray or CT technology.

Radioactive Reactions

By examining X-ray films, CT scans, and MRIs, doctors can generally get pictures of the structure of the nervous system, but not the functioning of it. Nuclear medicine uses radioactive materials and computers to produce moving, real-time images. These pictures allow doctors to evaluate both the structure and function of the nervous system. This special testing is used to help detect tumors, aneurysms, irregular blood flow, and functional disorders of certain organs.

One nuclear-medicine technique is called positron emission tomography (PET). A PET scanner is a donut-shaped machine that contains a gamma ray detector. A patient is ad-

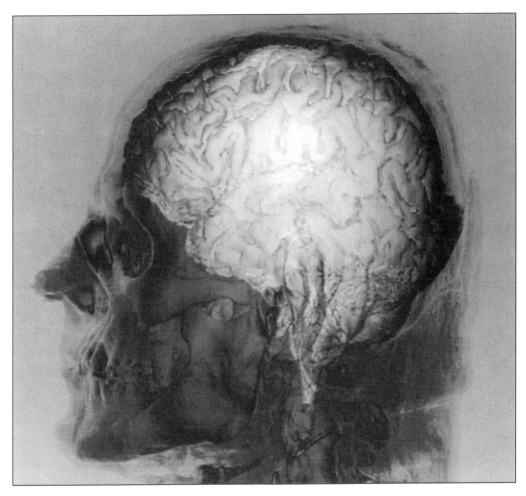

ministered a small amount of a radioactive material, either by injection or as a tablet to be swallowed. As the radioactive substance travels through the patient's bloodstream, it releases charged particles called positrons, which are detected by the scanner. The scanner converts the energy of the positrons into electrical signals that are sent to a computer, where images are generated.

The resulting images look like thin, living slices of the brain in action. They are moving, three-dimensional pictures that reveal not only structure but also brain processes such as blood flow, glucose breakdown, and oxygen consumption. PET scans provide invaluable information about

The combination of CT and MRI scans provides this three-dimensional view of the brain.

the brains of people who have had a stroke or who have epilepsy or brain tumors. PET scans also show the effects of certain drugs on the brain. Due to the small number of machines in the United States and the high cost of conducting a PET scan, this technology is not used as often as other imaging systems.

Charting Brain Waves

The use of electroencephalography to measure electrical activity in the brain is one of the oldest tests in neurology. To produce an EEG, sixteen to twenty-five electrodes are attached to the patient's scalp to detect the brain's electrical activity. The brain's electrical impulses are carried to an electroencephalograph, which magnifies them and then records them as a series of wavy lines.

During the EEG procedure, the patient is comfortably arranged in a bed or reclining chair. The patient is then asked to relax with eyes closed. In this resting position, brain waves are recorded to establish a baseline of data. Baseline brain waves are used as a comparison for brain waves produced when outside stimuli are introduced. The patient is then exposed to stimuli such as flashing lights and loud noises.

Brain waves called alpha, beta, theta, and delta, after letters in the Greek alphabet, are known to have typical frequencies and rhythms that are dependent on mental alertness, the physical condition of the brain, and outside stimuli. Some neurological conditions produce characteristic brain-wave patterns. Patients with epilepsy often show abnormally large, spiked brain waves, whereas those with brain tumors or lesions display very slow frequency delta brain waves that are normally only seen in people during sleep. Sometimes the effectiveness of a medication on brain activity is evaluated by comparing brain waves before and after taking the medication. The absence of any waves, the well-known flat-line pattern, indicates that there is no electrical activity.

Electromyography (EMG) is another type of electrical activity test. In this technique, small needles are placed in muscles to record their electrical activity. The electrical activity is recorded as photographs from the display of waves on an oscilloscope or as tracings on special recording paper. Normal resting muscle has no electrical activity. Even a slight muscular contraction produces some electrical activity. As contractions increase in intensity, so does the electrical activity. EMG helps diagnose diseases of the muscular,

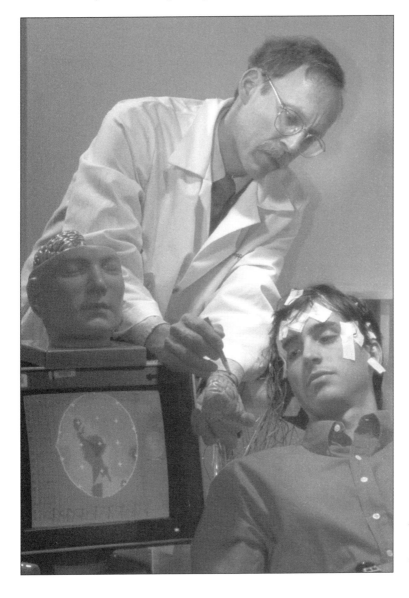

A technician explains to a patient how an EEG works.

peripheral, and spinal motor neurons, since these conditions cause abnormal electrical activity.

Testing in the Lab

Doctors also use laboratory tests to gather information about patients. Examination of cerebrospinal fluid can help detect neurological infections such as meningitis as well as vascular accidents such as stroke. The procedure called a lumbar puncture, or spinal tap, is used to withdraw cerebrospinal fluid by means of a hollow needle inserted between the third and fourth lumbar vertebrae. When examined visually, a normal sample of cerebrospinal fluid is a clear liquid. Cloudy fluid may point to infection, and bloody fluid may indicate brain hemorrhage. Laboratory testing on the fluid sample can show if its chemical makeup is within normal limits. Cerebrospinal fluid normally contains only small amounts of glucose and protein. High levels of protein in the fluid can suggest the presence of tumors, while low levels may indicate meningitis infection. Samples of the cerebrospinal fluid are cultured in the lab to test for presence of disease-causing microorganisms. Since normal fluid will not support the growth of any microorganisms, their presence in cultured fluid indicates infection.

Tools and Techniques

By using the tools and techniques available, neurologists are usually able to diagnose the illnesses that trouble their patients. The next step for the doctor and patient is the development of a successful treatment plan. Like diagnostic work, treatments also take advantage of many innovative technologies. Sometimes surgery is the treatment of choice for a neurological disorder. New technology has advanced the field of surgery to include microsurgery, neuro-navigational surgery, stereotactic radiosurgery, and robotic surgery.

The development of microsurgery is often lauded as the advance that brought high technology into the world of neurosurgery. The technological revolution in neuro-surgery began in the 1960s when a magnifying device called the operating microscope was designed for use in delicate surgeries. The first doctors to use this binocular instrument were surgeons of the eye and ear. Later neurosurgeons found that the operating microscope provided an improved level of magnification and light that enabled them to re-move tiny lesions and tumors that were once considered in-operable.

The operating microscope contains an optical system for both eyes. During surgery, the instrument is positioned on a stand above the operating field. The surgeon can move the microscope up and down using a foot pedal. Under the operating microscope, the surgeon can see the finest details with great clarity. Neurosurgeons often use miniaturized tools known as microinstruments. By acting like exten-sions of the surgeon's hands, the operating microscope and microinstruments allow the repair of aneurysms in the brain, the removal of ruptured discs from the spine, and the excision of brain tumors without damaging surrounding tissue.

After a tumor is removed, further treatment may be needed to ensure that it does not grow back. The advent of stereotactic radiosurgery provided a way for doctors to kill or shrink tumor cells without damaging the healthy surround-ing tissue. Stereotactic radiosurgery, which delivers a con-centrated dose of radiation to the tumor area, can even reach deep-seated tumors that may not be accessible by other means.

Radiosurgery

Unlike traditional surgery, radiosurgery does not require an incision. An MRI or CT scan is performed prior to the pro-cedure to confirm the exact location of the tumor. The doctor enters data into a computer, designating the location and size of the tumor and the amount of radiation that will be used to treat it. The patient is placed on a table and fitted with a metal helmet. The helmet helps direct radiation to the correct area, while protecting other parts of the brain. A linear accelerator provides low-intensity radiation to the designated spot in the patient's head. The goal of this relatively pain-free procedure is to deliver enough radiation to destroy the tumor without damaging the healthy tissue that surrounds it.

Image-Guided Surgery

In the past, MRIs and CT scans were almost exclusively used for diagnostic purposes. But today they also serve as navigation instruments during operations on the brain. In the technique of image-guided surgery, cameras mounted above the operating table provide three-dimensional pictures of the brain on a monitor that can be viewed by the surgeon. As soon as a surgical instrument touches the patient, its location is superimposed on the image of the brain appearing on the monitor. During the course of the surgery, different views of the brain are constantly pictured on the monitor. This real-time imaging technique allows surgeons to navigate around healthy tissue safely so that hard-to-reach tumors can be removed with minimal damage to the rest of the brain.

Robotic Surgery

Even with the technologies that enhance surgical procedures, there is always a potential for human error. As surgeons tire during a long surgery, their arms and hands can develop slight tremors. For this reason, robotic-assisted microsurgery (RAMS) may be an option for the future. This new technology developed by NASA is now being used to perform surgical procedures on laboratory animals. Thus far, RAMS has played only a minimal role in surgery on humans. However, scientists predict that one day these machines will be able to perform major surgical procedures.

RAMS will still require the guidance of a human surgeon. The actions of the robot may be dictated in a variety of ways, ranging from voice activation to manipulation of joystick-like devices on a console. The FDA recently ap-

proved the use of the first robotic device, called the da Vinci System, in American operating rooms. This system has a viewing and control console along with a surgical arm. The surgeon manipulates the controls on the console much as a person would use the joystick in a video game. As the surgeon moves the controls manually, signals sent to da Vinci's computer enable it to instruct the robot to move the surgical instrument in sync with the movements of the surgeon. Since the computer has been programmed to compensate for any tremors of the surgeon's hands, such unwanted motions are ignored, and the mechanical arm remains steady. There are several other robotic devices

A doctor sitting at a workstation demonstrates the da Vinci surgical system, the first robotic device capable of providing surgical assistance.

presently awaiting approval for use in the United States. Experts believe the advent of these devices will add safety and precision to operations and eliminate the need for large teams of surgeons in a room during the course of one operation.

New Cells Offer New Chances

The brain and spinal cord are made of neurons, cells that generally do not grow or reproduce. As a result, injuries to nervous tissue can be devastating. For example, damage to normal, functioning cells in the brain due to head injury or disease can cause loss of speech, mobility, or memory. Injury to the spinal cord can result in partial or total lack of function in areas such as the legs, arms, bladder, and bowels.

However, research in cell-based therapies is making some remarkable advances. For example, in some experimental labs, scientists have successfully stimulated growth in nerve cells. As a result, nerve cells reestablish connections with each other in the brains and spinal cords of experimental animals. This line of work gives hope to many people with brain and spinal cord injuries.

On a different front, research on the transplant of cells into damaged nervous systems is promising. Very few neurological diseases respond well to drug therapies. Traditionally, Parkinson's disease has been treated by providing a supplement of the chemical L-dopa, the precursor of dopamine, to brain cells that are not able to produce the neurotransmitter. However, over time, L-dopa becomes ineffective and its side effects debilitating. An alternative therapy is to supply the damaged brain of a Parkinson's patient with new, healthy cells to replace the damaged ones.

Experiments on rats, mice, and pigs show that implanted neurons can form new synapses, secrete neurotransmitters, and take over the functions of dead cells. Cells implanted into lab animals are injected directly into the damaged areas of the brain. The number of cells that must be transplanted to produce results is very small, only one-tenth of a million of the total number of nerve cells in the brain. In other research, transplanted cells have healed areas of spinal cord damage. Studies done on cats show that transplants helped 40 percent of the animals with spinal cord damage regain at least some mobility.

Cells used in replacement therapy must be able to give rise to many cell types. This ability is called pluripotency. When pluripotent cells are implanted in a tissue, they develop into that same type of tissue: pluripotent cells injected in the brains of animals with Parkinson's disease become healthy, dopamine-producing cells; those inserted in a damaged part of the spinal cord become spinal-cord tissue.

There are only a few potential sources of pluripotent cells. One of the most controversial is fetal cells, removed from the nerve tissue of aborted fetuses. Another source of pluripotent cells are embryos that are created from the union of an egg cell and another cell in the laboratory. Some labs are working on techniques for growing pluripotent cells in cultures that can be maintained in the lab. Given the promise of pluripotent cells in the development of new therapies, scientists are working around the clock to find a source of cells that will be acceptable from a bioethical standpoint as well as medically functional.

The Final Word

The body could not function without a nervous system. This communication network receives information about the internal and external environments and reacts to that information appropriately. By doing so, it manages the entire body.

The nervous system is made up of billions of nerve cells, or neurons, and their support system. Neurons have the unique ability to create and transmit electrical impulses through the body. These impulses carry messages to and from the brain, the system's central command post.

Because the nervous system controls all functions, conditions that damage it can produce symptoms in any part of the body. Infections, degenerative diseases, injuries, and drugs are a few of the mechanisms that can impair neurological function. Today's high-tech world provides physicians with an arsenal of advanced neurological treatments and diagnostic equipment. Advanced imaging techniques such as CT scans, MRIs, PET scans, and nuclear-medicine imaging have greatly improved the view inside the human body. Aided by EEGs and EMGs, physicians can study the electrical activity in the brain, muscles, and nerves. Laboratory analysis of blood and cerebrospinal

The elegant neuron serves as the foundation for the myriad activities of the nervous system.

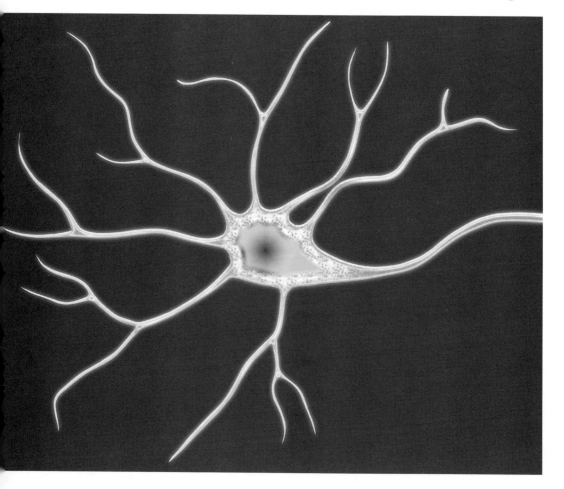

fluid help detect infections and diseases that once could not be identified.

Some of the treatments available today were mere science-fiction fantasies in the middle of the twentieth century. Radiosurgery, microsurgery, image-guided surgery, and robotic surgery have increased the range of procedures, making them safer and more precise. Research to develop methods for replacing injured nerve cells with new cells gives hope to those who suffer neurological damage.

GLOSSARY

axon: An extension of a neuron that carries nerve impulses to other cells.

brain stem: The section of the brain that includes the medulla oblongata, pons, and midbrain.

cerebellum: The portion of the brain that controls movements.

cerebrospinal fluid: A clear fluid formed in the ventricles of the brain that bathes the brain and spinal cord.

cerebrum: The uppermost portion of the brain that is in charge of higher mental functions.

dendrite: An extension of a neuron that receives nerve impulses from other cells.

diencephalon: The middle portion of the brain that contains the thalamus and hypothalamus.

electroencephalogram (EEG): A recording of the electrical activity of brain waves.

enzyme: A protein that speeds up chemical reactions within a cell.

gray matter: The area of the central nervous system that lacks myelin.

limbic system: Several interrelated areas in the brain that work together to produce emotions.

magnetic resonance imaging (MRI): A technique for visualizing internal structures using energy released by magnetic fields.

meninges: Membranes that cover the brain and spinal cord.

myelin: Fatty material that provides a sheath-like cover on some neurons.

neuron: A cell specialized to generate and carry electrical impulses in the body.

neuroglia: Tissue composed of cells that nourish and support neurons.

neurotransmitter: A chemical secreted at the axon end of a neuron that carries an impulse across a synapse.

receptor cell: Sensory cell that can detect and transmit sensory stimuli.

sensory adaptation: A reduction in the rate at which nerve impulses are generated by sensory receptors that are exposed to continuous stimulation.

synapse: The gap between a neuron and another cell that is bridged by a neurotransmitter.

ventricles: Spaces within the brain.

vitreous humor: Gel-like fluid that fills the anterior chamber of the eye.

white matter: The area of the central nervous system that contains myelin.

FOR FURTHER READING

Books

Jim Barmeier, *The Brain*. San Diego, CA: Lucent Books, 1996. This book reviews historical and current understanding of brain structure, memory, sleep, diseases, and treatments.

Charles B. Clayman, *The Brain and Nervous System.* Pleasantville, NY: Reader's Digest Association, 1991. This book provides general information on anatomy and functions of the nervous system, including consciousness and sleep.

Jack Fincher, *The Brain*. Washington, DC: U.S. News Books, nd. After reviewing brain anatomy and function, this book focuses on how drugs affect the brain.

Alma Guinness, *ABC's of the Human Body.* Pleasantville, NY: Reader's Digest Association, 1987. This book discusses the various structures of the human body and addresses some interesting reasons for certain body functions.

The Handy Science Answer Book. Canton, MI: Visible Ink Press, 1997. This book gives good explanations for a variety of happenings in the science world.

How in the World? Pleasantville, NY: Reader's Digest Association, 1990. This book provides interesting coverage of both physical and biological events that occur in life.

David E. Larson, *Mayo Clinic Family Health Book.* New York: William Morrow, 1996. This book describes in simple terms the many diseases that can affect the human body.

Susan McKeever, *The Dorling Kindersley Science Encyclopedia.* New York: Dorling Kindersley, 1994. This encyclopedia gives concise information on physical and biological occurrences in life. Good illustrations help to explain topics.

Mary Lou Mulvihill, *Human Diseases.* Norwalk, CT: Appleton and Lange, 1995. This book provides a good description of the most common diseases of the human body.

Lael Wertenbaker, *The Eye.* Washington, DC: U.S. News Books, nd. A comprehensive explanation of the eye and its functions.

World Book Medical Encyclopedia. Chicago: World Book, 1995. This encyclopedia provides a vast amount of information on the physiology of human body systems.

Websites

Countdown for Kids Magazine (www.jdf.org). Students can research any topic that interests them, including health and medicine.

Fact Monster, Learning (www.factmonster.com). This website provides information on a wide variety of topics and has a good science encyclopedia.

Neuroscience for Kids (http://faculty.washington.edu) Information, experiments, activities, and research links on the nervous system are available at this site.

Yucky Kids (www.nj.com). Easy-to-read articles on the nervous system and other body systems.

WORKS CONSULTED

Books

Robert Berkow, *The Merck Manual of Medical Information*. New York: Pocket Books, 1997. Provides a detailed explanation of all organs. This book gives information on the causes, symptoms, diagnosis, and treatment of many diseases.

Brain Facts: A Primer on the Brain and Nervous System. Washington, DC: Society for Neuroscience, 1993. Outlines the physiology of parts of the nervous system and presents current knowledge on memory, sleep, and diseases of the nervous system.

Charlotte Dienhart, *Basic Human Anatomy and Physiology*. Philadelphia: W.B. Saunders, 1979. This textbook covers the structure and function of all organ systems in the human body. It also provides information on symptoms and treatments of various diseases.

William C. Goldberg, *Clinical Physiology Made Ridiculously Simple*. Miami: Med Masters, 1995. This booklet gives a detailed explanation of body systems. Illustrations reinforce the written content.

John Hole Jr., *Essentials of Human Anatomy and Physiology*. Dubuque, IA: Wm. C. Brown, 1992. This textbook of anatomy and physiology provides detailed explanations of the structure and function of all human body systems.

Anthony L. Komaroff, *Harvard Medical School Family Health Guide*. New York: Simon and Schuster, 1999. This book provides comprehensive coverage of the various disorders and diseases that can affect the human body. Symptoms, causes, diagnosis, and treatment options are provided.

Ann Kramer, *The Human Body. The World Book Encyclopedia of Science*. Chicago: World Book, 1987. This book provides information on all body systems and gives explanations about unusual and interesting events that occur in the human body.

Peretz Lavie, *The Enchanted World of Sleep*. New Haven and London: Yale University Press, 1996. The author explains current and past studies on sleep, giving the reader a complete picture of sleep research.

Stanley Loeb, *The Illustrated Guide to Diagnostic Tests*. Springhouse, PA: Springhouse Corporation, 1994. This medical book gives a thorough description and explanation of how and why medical technologies are employed to diagnose and treat human diseases and disorders.

Elaine Marieb, *Human Anatomy and Physiology*. Redwood City, CA: Benjamin/Cummings, 1995. This book offers a detailed explanation of all human body structures and organs.

Lawrence Pool, *Nature's Masterpiece: The Brain and How It Works*. New York: Walker, 1987. This book contains concise descriptions of each part of the brain and the roles neurosurgeons play in advancing the knowledge of brain function.

Richard Restak, *The Brain*. New York: Bantam Books, 1984. Based on the PBS television series of the same name, this book provides a comprehensive review of brain structure and function.

———, *Receptors*. New York: Bantam Books, 1994. This book describes recent scientific advances in mapping brain function and research on the effects of drugs on brain cells.

Websites

About (www.about.com). This is an easy-to-use website that offers information on a wide variety of topics, including health and medicine.

American Association of Neurological Surgeons (www.neuro surgery.org). This website describes research and treatments for patients with brain tumors.

CDC (www.cdc.gov). This website contains information from the Centers for Disease Control and Prevention on any topic in health.

Clinical Implications (www.nobel.se). This website contains drawings and photographs along with information on all medical topics.

Cornell Medical College (www.edcenter.med.cornell.edu). The medical college of Cornell provides a wide range of information on body systems.

11th Hour (www.blackwellscience.com). This is a valuable resource for any type of information in science. To find information on the nervous system, go to "Introduction to Biology."

JAMA HIV AIDS Resource Center (www.ama-assn.org). The *Journal of the American Medical Association,* published by the American Medical Association, is a great resource for any topic in medicine.

Michigan Parkinson Foundation (http://parkinsonsmi.org). The Parkinson Foundation of Michigan gives a good overview of what Parkinson's disease is, who gets it, the symptoms and treatments, and how to cope with the disease.

MSN Search (www.search.msn.com). This website provides a science library suitable for most students.

New England Neurological Associates (www.neneuro.com). This website provides the latest advances in neurosurgery and explains how brain tumors can be treated by microsurgery, laser techniques, and radioactive implants.

The Merck Manual Web Site (www.merck.com). This website gives a detailed explanation of body systems and diseases.

Internet Sources

American Heart Association, "Stroke Treatment Advances," 2000. www.americanheart.org.

Dr. Koop Lifecare Corporation, "Robotics and Surgery of the Brain and Spinal Cord," April 11, 2000. www.drkoop.com.

Encarta Online Encyclopedia, "Coma," November 4, 2001. http://encarta.msn.com.

Gale Encyclopedia of Medicine, "Cerebrospinal Fluid Analysis." www.findarticles.com.

———, "Electrical Stimulation of the Brain." www.findarticles.com.

———, "Evoked Potential Studies." www.findarticles.com.

Health Alliance, "World's First Optimized Stereotactic Radiotherapy System in the Neuroscience Institute at the University Hospital of Cincinnati," August 5, 2001. www.techmall.com.

How Stuff Works, "How Magnetic Resonance Imaging Works," 2001. www.howstuffworks.com.

———, "How Robotic Surgery Will Work." 2001. www.howstuff works.com.

International Radiosurgery Support Association, "A Typical Treatment Day: Information on Gamma Knife and Linac Stereotactic Radiosurgery for Brain Tumors," 2000. www.irsa.org.

Methodist Health Care System, "Infectious Diseases," 2001. www.methodisthealth.com.

New York State Department of Health Communicable Disease Fact Sheet, "Tetanus," February 1999. www.health.state.ny.us.

Society for Neuroscience, "Brain Imaging," 1996. www.sfn.org.

INDEX

acetylcholine, 17, 66, 68
adaptation, 29, 40
alcohol, 12, 76–77
Alzheimer, Alois, 67
Alzheimer's disease, 66–68
amygdala, 19
angiography, 82
antibiotics, 62, 65
anticonvulsants, 70
anvil, 36–37
aqueous humor, 34
arachnoid membrane, 21
arterial blockage, 72
autonomic nervous system,
  23–25
axons, 12

balance, 18, 23
 see also equilibrium
basal ganglia, 20, 68
biological clock, 51
biological rhythm, 19
blood chemistry, 24, 25
blood clot, 72
blood pressure, 24, 25
body temperature, 19
brain
  alcohol and, 76–77
  cavities in, 21
  central processing function,
    25–26
  characteristics of, 17–18
  diagram of parts, 19

diseases of. See names of specific
  diseases
fluid of, 21
fluid of. function of, 17
lobes of, 20–21
membranes of, 21
neurons in, 18
oxygen and, 72
protective system of, 21, 60
sections of, 18
unconscious, 18
ventricles of, 21
brain contusion, 70
brain damage, 70, 72
brain scans, 82–86
brain stem, 18
brain tumors, 70, 73–75, 89–90
brain waves, 51–53, 86
breathing, 24, 25
Broca's area, 20

cartilage, 22
cell membrane, 11
cell transplant, 92–93
central nervous system, 17–22
 see also nervous system
cerebellum, 18
cerebral angiography, 82
cerebral cortex, 20, 40, 50
cerebrospinal fluid (CSF), 21,
  62, 88
cerebrum, 18, 20, 41, 68
chemoreceptors, 29

PICTURE CREDITS

ABOUT THE AUTHORS

Both Pam Walker and Elaine Wood have degrees in biology and education from colleges in Georgia. They have taught science in grades seven through twelve since the mid-1980s. Ms. Walker and Ms. Wood are coauthors of more than a dozen resource and activity books for science teachers and two science textbooks.